D1212539

America's First Freedom Rider

America's First Freedom Rider

Elizabeth Jennings, Chester A. Arthur, and the Early Fight for Civil Rights

Jerry Mikorenda

Guilford, Connecticut

An imprint of The Rowman & Littlefield Publishing Group, Inc.
4501 Forbes Blvd., Ste. 200
Lanham, MD 20706
www.rowman.com

Distributed by NATIONAL BOOK NETWORK

British Library Cataloguing in Publication Information available

Library of Congress Control Number Available
ISBN 978-1-4930-4134-3 (hardcover)
ISBN 978-1-4930-4135-0 (e-book)

∞™ The paper used in this publication meets the minimum requirements of American National Standard for Information Sciences—Permanence of Paper for Printed Library Materials, ANSI/NISO Z39.48-1992.

To my angels, Camille and Gabrielle,
whose wings lift me every day

Contents

Preface: Unheralded Labors

Truth uncompromisingly told will always have its ragged edges.
—Herman Melville,
Billy Budd

Mass transportation is the uninvited guest in the lives of city dwellers.

He keeps them up at night with his clanking and hissing, disrupts their meals, causes them to miss family outings, and is always looking for money. Surely life would be better if he just went away. If only for a day or so.

On October 29, 2012, New Yorkers got their wish. Superstorm Sandy swallowed the city whole, drowning its tunnels, railways, and buses. For days afterward not much worked. Transportation was at a standstill. Suddenly getting to a job, crossing town, or going to an event was a major undertaking.

The city's uninvited guest was quirky, temperamental, and a bit slovenly, but Manhattanites knew him well. He was the guy everyone loved to hate. One could imagine Joni Mitchell humming "Big Yellow Taxi" as Gothamites chased after the few big yellow taxis in town.

This small dose of transit-less-ness gave rise to a thought. What if a whole class of people today were excluded from using public transportation after everything returned to a New York normal? How would that diminish their lives, affect where they work, reduce their ability to get Wi-Fi, and limit the schools their kids attended? Would we call it sound business, say it's not my concern, or shout in outrage?

That shows in a relatable twenty-first-century way just how important it was, and how much was at stake, 165 years ago when *Elizabeth Jennings v. Third Avenue Railroad Company* was on the docket in the New York State Supreme Court in Brooklyn.

Unequal treatment of individuals, even when it comes to nuisance issues that we all roll our eyes about every day, matters. Although Ms. Jennings never took a Pilates class, didn't have a Facebook page or a Twitter account to share her thoughts, I believe that deep down she understood the connectivity that small acts of heroism provide.

It would've been easy to back off that horse-drawn streetcar on July 16, 1854, as the conductor wanted her to do and grouse about missing church choir over the dinner table as many of us might have. But she didn't.

Traveling in those days was full of danger. Omnibus accidents were commonplace. Earlier in 1854 one claimed the life of twelve-year-old Daniel Moran. He was run over by the wheels of an omnibus as he pulled a handcart near Ninth Avenue. Pedestrians were mugged or beaten in the middle of the day by Five Points gangs. Rival police forces watched and argued over who should help. Pickpockets, drunks, and kidnappers were all part of the daily street scene in old New York. It was a sinister and harsh place for many of its citizens. They endured and transformed a trading post into the Empire City.

Any female walking a Manhattan street by herself after dusk risked being arrested and jailed. The charge was either vagrancy or prostitution. In 1855, Matilda Wade left her home on Clark Street in Manhattan to meet her husband at his job a few blocks away. It was a warm spring evening around eight when she was abruptly grabbed by a policeman and placed under arrest for prostitution and vagrancy. She was brought with nineteen other women to the Eighth Ward station house. She spent five days jailed in the Tombs and on Blackwell's Island.

According to the April 2, 1855, edition of the *New York Times*, her husband demanded a writ of habeas corpus and produced an affidavit from her stating "that she never had any trial and no opportunity to employ counsel, or even to send for her husband." Wade was one of forty-one women from ages sixteen to forty arrested in the Eighth and Fourteenth Precincts that night. Eventually charges were dismissed against thirty of the women, including Wade. At least one was pulled off a streetcar similar to the one Elizabeth was attempting to get on. Those women not as lucky as Wade were convicted without a trial, witness, or lawyer. Many resorted to dressing as men if they had to traverse the city alone.

None of this was on Elizabeth's mind as she climbed the platform onto the Chatham Street horsecar. We can only imagine the sense of relief she anticipated when she could settle into her seat. But her destination and that of the country took a sudden turn when the conductor told her to wait for the next car because it had "her people" in it.

It's a refrain that still echoes today—Elizabeth's "people" were African Americans. This is the story of what happened that day. It's also the story about her family, the struggle for equality, and race relations. It's the history of America at its most despicable and most exhilarating. Yet few historians know of Elizabeth Jennings or the impact she had on desegregating public transit.

For many people that movement began with Rosa Parks. Even though the events that tie Jennings and Parks together happened a century apart, the two women are contemporaries. Freedom riders both, they are bonded by single acts of defiance. One was a twenty-seven-year-old schoolteacher

Elizabeth Jennings about the time of her trial in 1855.
WIKIMEDIA COMMONS

going to church to play the organ. The other was a forty-two-year-old coming home from work as a seamstress. Both women just wanted to get where they were going. Each ended up in a very different place.

Parks, rightfully so, is still celebrated as an iconic figure of the civil rights movement. Claudette Colvin, the Montgomery, Alabama, teenager who preceded her, is also acknowledged for her role in 1950s transit integration. Parks and Colvin were on the bus in large part because Elizabeth won her case one hundred years before them.

Elizabeth Jennings's saga spans the breadth of American history from the Revolution to today. The entire Jennings family used their skills to end slavery's grip upon this nation.

That grip couldn't have been stronger than it was in the 1850s. The *Dred Scott* decision, *Roberts v. Boston*, and the Fugitive Slave Act all painted a bleak picture for African Americans hoping to obtain their natural right to equal citizenship and social standing.

The young attorney who defended Elizabeth—Chester A. Arthur—would become the twenty-first president of the United States. His fame brought a renewed interest in Jennings's old lawsuit. Unfortunately, rather than show how far the United States had come in its race relations, it illustrated just how far the country had fallen. Arthur's and Jennings's lives paralleled and intertwined over the years before and after the trial that bound them together. The result holds a mirror to the norms of a society that to this day values race and gender over all other attributes. Despite being born into poverty, Arthur rose to the highest office in the land. As a female of color, Jennings had to fight every day for some semblance of human rights.

America's First Freedom Rider: Elizabeth Jennings, Chester A. Arthur, and the Early Fight for Civil Rights brings together the cultural and historical events surrounding her life. It places national issues in the context of her time, her family, her story. It's an age not unlike our own, fraught with racism, partisan politics, and the struggles for marginalized groups to gain equal status.

In an 1859 newspaper tribute that marked the passing of Elizabeth's father, Frederick Douglass wrote, "He was not an exception, but a representative of his class whose noble sacrifices and unheralded labors are too little known to the public."

This book is the total of many efforts over the years to bring those labors into proper focus as part of the American diorama—ragged edges and all.

Chapter I

Good Old New York Stock

On the day when race prejudice ran so high among us, it is well to recall the story among other patriotic and heroic deeds.

—H. Cordelia Ray,
"The Story of an Old Wrong"

On Sunday, July 16, 1854, temperatures hovered near one hundred degrees. New York City was in the midst of a crippling heat wave. Work in the shipyards stopped. Sunstroke and "brain fever" caused dozens of deaths. Horses dropped in the streets from the swelter.

For Elizabeth Jennings, the heat wave wasn't as brutal as her wardrobe. Properly dressed females wore up to seven layers of floor-length petticoats. They also put on corsets before adding a two-piece outer dress, gloves, and a hat. It was hard to walk, let alone chase after a horse-drawn streetcar in such garb.

The schoolteacher and her friend Sarah E. Adams were on their way to church services. That spring Elizabeth became the organist and choir leader for the First Colored American Congregational Church. These were both unusual occupations for a woman at the time.

Located at the corner of Sixth Street and Second Avenue, the church was about two miles from where she lived with her parents. Walking down Pearl Street, they passed Bailey & Brothers, offering carpeting, flooring, and oilcloths. John Willard's Looking Glasses & Picture Frames shop came next. They stopped at the corner of Chatham Street to wait for a bus.

Standing there, Elizabeth saw a horsecar slowly making its way uptown. The two women knew it wasn't the car they usually took. Elizabeth probably felt lucky one was coming at all. On Sundays many of the omnibuses had only a driver. He was too busy to care who got on and off. Conductors, on the other hand, had the time and opportunity to deny patrons entrance if they wished.

The light green bus appeared half full as Elizabeth waved to flag it down. The deafening sound of the iron wheels scraping along metal track ceased. In one motion Elizabeth swung herself up onto the iron platform. While she waited for Sarah, the conductor approached her.

No one knows Elizabeth Jennings's actual birth date. At one time, it was generally accepted that she was born in 1830 because that was the first US Census she appeared in. However, in the 1900 Census, a year before she died, Elizabeth listed her age as seventy-three but crossed out a date that appears. Her 1901 death certificate reports her age as seventy-four, which would place her birth during 1827. She took the actual date with her to the grave.

The Jennings family had deep roots in Manhattan that predated the American Revolution, with many members of the family born and raised there. Years later, Frederick Douglass would refer to their lineage as "good old New York Stock." That stock began with her grandfather Jacob Cartwright, who served admirably in the Continental Army during the American Revolution. Many African Americans earned their freedom by serving as Washington's minutemen. However, many others were denied the equality promised to them.

In the 1800 Census, Cartwright was listed as a free black. He lived on Duane and Anthony Streets for many years in homes owned or rented by Elizabeth's father. It was a part of the city built on a filled-in pond. The intersection where all the streets met gave the area its infamous nickname—the Five Points. It was home to tanneries, rope makers, and various other "malodorous" industries. During the 1870s the city Board of Health produced stench maps to identify these offending neighborhoods. By then Brooklyn was the big culprit with its "offensive trades," at a time when many thought odors caused disease.

The Five Points became a landing place for the city's poor. Its diverse population also made it one of America's first melting pots. "The Points" was a world unto itself. Within its confines, African Americans could hold

The infamous Five Points was one of America's first melting pots.
COURTESY NEW YORK PUBLIC LIBRARY

local office, vote, and campaign for their candidates. In 1815, New York state passed a law requiring free blacks to show special permits to vote. Six years later other voting limits were added, including an increase in the property required for black men to vote from one hundred to two hundred fifty dollars. (This was eliminated for whites.)

Elizabeth's grandfather was active in city politics throughout his long life. Cartwright died on April 23, 1824. He was buried in the First Baptist Cemetery in Manhattan.

The area also attracted other trades and men of ambition. In 1807, a sixteen-year-old freeborn native New Yorker, Thomas L. Jennings, became an apprentice to one of the city's finest tailors. During this time Jennings courted Elizabeth Cartwright and was seen parading through the streets with the sign Am I not a Man and a Brother? He participated in many neighborhood street celebrations over the years.

Jennings wed Elizabeth Cartwright and opened a tailor shop on Williams Street at age nineteen. Two years later he was listed in the city's reverse directory as a merchant tailor at 23 Cortlandt Street, meaning he was able to sell the clothes he created from fabric. Many tailors only altered existing outfits. It was a cutthroat business. Other tailors looked to Jennings for work. Military uniforms cost about $13; men's pantaloons $1.50, plus 37½ cents more for garters at the knee. Cloaks went for $5.

Around 1810, the Jennings eldest child, William, was born. He was followed by another son, Thomas Jr., and three daughters, Matilda, Sarah, and Elizabeth. Elizabeth was much younger than her brothers and sisters. Nearly twenty years separated her from William. As the youngest, Elizabeth must have been raised in part by her four older siblings. Their retelling of family stories and the examples they set must have helped forge her moral compass.

Before Elizabeth and her sisters were born, more-urgent needs replaced life's everyday concerns. In August 1814, a fleet of five British warships attacked nearby Stonington, Connecticut, bringing the War of 1812 to New York City's doorstep. Revolutionary War veterans such as Jacob Cartwright must have recalled the Battle of Long Island and the city's long siege under British occupation with the dreaded prison barges anchored off of Kip's Bay and the Brooklyn shoreline. City leaders asked for fortifications and trenches from Harlem Heights to Brooklyn. A proclamation was issued calling for

> *All who feel that they possess a country to defend and love, should step forward with a degree of zeal and alacrity, which shall touch the enemy, and convince the world that America is a virtuous, great, and united nation.*

Within days the city's trade groups responded. Members of the Master Butchers Association, Mechanics' Society, and Sons of Erin volunteered for duty. Thomas Jennings was among the "one thousand citizens of color from the city of New York" dispatched to fortify Brooklyn and dig trenches to defend the region. The *Long Island Star* reported that the recruits arrived to "flourishes of music and the roar of applause from thousands of cheering voices."

Lacking a national song, resident Samuel Woodworth wrote a tune distributed for all to sing as they worked. "The Patriotic Diggers" captured the mood of the times.

> To protect our rights
> 'Gainst your flints and triggers,
> See on Brooklyn Heights
> Our patriotic diggers;
> Men of every age,
> Color, rank, profession,
> Ardently engage
> Labor in succession

Blacks and Irish toiled side by side with lawyers and indentured servants. The equality promised by the ideals of the American Revolution seemed finally to be within their grasp. Residents were armed and waiting, but the expected siege never came. On February 20, 1815, church bells rang out throughout Manhattan and Brooklyn. Inhabitants of the two cities celebrated the peace treaty with bonfires, parades, and parties into the night.

With two baby boys and another child on the way, Jennings now understood there was a price for freedom that each generation must accept. As his business flourished, he continued his activism and community leadership. On more than one occasion, he signed "Certificates of Freedom" or "Affidavits of Freedom" in which he pledged that the African American holder was a free person. Such certificates described the holder's physical appearance. They were used by blacks to travel in slave states, as identification, and to vote if the holder was eligible. Each document was also countersigned by a white city official. According to historian Sarah Gronningsater, the certificates cost 37½ cents to register, plus filing fees with the city. The cost of these certificates and the obstacle of finding a man willing to sign an affidavit for the holder as well as a white city official to sign off on the certificate deterred blacks from voting.

In December 1812, Jennings signed an affidavit for city resident Henry Parson's Certificate of Freedom. He also signed another in March 1814 for a John Johnson. In both instances he was vouching for their status as free men and clearly signed his name as "Thos L. Jinnings." This has led to confusion about his identify over the years, as "Jinnings" and "Jennings" were used interchangeably in newspaper accounts.

City and County of New-York, ss. Thomas L. Jennings
of the fifth Ward, of the said city, being duly sworn saith that he has for four years last past, been well acquainted with Henry Parsons
a black or mulatto man, that the said Henry
resides in the said city, that he is about the age of Thirty years, and was born at Richmond
in Virginia as this deponent is informed and verily believes, that during all the said time whilst this deponent has been acquainted with the said
Henry as aforesaid, the said Henry
hath been reputed and considered to be free, and hath continually acted as a free man during the said time, and that the said
Henry was born free [illegible]

as this deponent is also informed and believes. And further this deponent saith not.

SWORN *the* Sixteenth *day of* December 1812 *Before me* — Thos L. Jinnings

Isaac S. Douglass Ald.

City and County of New-York, ss.

I Isaac S. Douglass
one of the Aldermen of the City of New-York, and a Judge of the Court of Commom pleas, called the Mayor's Court, in and for the [illegible]

Henry Parsons

residing in the said city, a black or mulatto
man exhibited proof before me, reduced to writing, of the freedom of him the said Henry and being satisfied with such proof, I am of opinion, and do adjudge that the said Henry

is free according to the laws of this State, and **I do further Certify,** that the said Henry
is a person about five feet eight inches high
has dark eyes and dark hair, that he is about the age of Thirty years, that he was born at Richmond
in Virginia and
that he was born free [illegible]

as nearly as the same can be ascertained.

GIVEN under my hand, this Sixteenth day of December in the year one thousand eight hundred and twelve

Isaac S. Douglass. ald.

Thomas L. Jennings signed this Certificate of Freedom for Henry Parsons in December 1812. COURTESY NEW-YORK HISTORICAL SOCIETY

By the early 1820s, Jennings owned one of the largest and best tailoring houses in the city. A shrewd businessman, he used his profits to buy or rent homes in the Five Points area. Tailors often gave work such as sewing and making buttonholes to their renters. It was the business model of the day. Entire families labored tirelessly stitching clothes in their cramped quarters. These home workers were called "sweaters" for the endless hours spent providing "sweat labor."

Another clothing-related job was "scouring," or cleaning. Clothes were ruined by ship tar, axle grease, and general filth. While hard work, it was a profitable business. Scouring shops sprang up all over the city with less than stellar results. The suit that was dropped off wasn't necessarily the one that came back. Holes appeared where stains once were. Clothing was discolored or totally ruined.

A master at his craft, Jennings was bothered to see his fine suits destroyed. He began experimenting with chemicals to clean fabrics without damaging them. By 1820, newspaper ads show he was offering this service to his customers.

CASH FOR CAST OFF CLOTHES.

WANTED to purchase a large quantity of cast-off Clothes, for which the highest price will be given by THOMAS L. JENNINGS, No. 110 Nassau-st., formerly No. 64; who has constantly on hand at the above place, a general assortment of second hand clothes, at the lowest prices for cash.

N. B. Those persons who wish to dispose of clothes, will please to send their address as above or send their articles before sun-set.

As this ad shows, using his dry scouring method, Thomas Jennings breathed new life into old clothes. *FREEDOM'S JOURNAL*, APRIL 6, 1827

On March 3, 1821, Jennings became the first African American to receive a patent from the US government. It was for the "exclusive right and liberty to the making, constructing, using and vending to others" the process of "Dry Scouring Clothes." A form of today's dry cleaning, it revolutionized the clothing industry. Ads in other cities proclaimed the wonders of this new technique. Jennings reaped the profits from his patent by receiving royalty payments.

LETTERS PATENT

BEING granted under the GREAT SEAL OF THE UNITED STATES OF AMERICA unto THOMAS L. JENNINGS, Tailor, 64 Nassau street, New-York, for his Invention of Dry Scouring Clothes, and Woollen Fabrics in general, so that they keep their original shape, and have the polish and appearance of new, Informs the public that he is ready to execute all Orders entrusted to him in the above line, on reasonable terms. He also Alters and Repairs Gentlemen's Clothes in the neatest manner, being regularly brought up to the Tailor's business, and practising in this city the last 14 years. He also removes stains from Cloth.

N.B. Directions will be given how Clothes may be kept in the condition they are delivered

☞ Gentlemen's Clothes purchased—Military Clothes and Accoutrements sold on Commission, on moderate terms. m8 1w

On Tuesday, March 13, 1821, the *New York Gazette* ran this announcement of Jennings's Letters of Patent. *NEW YORK GAZETTE*

Prior to 1836, the US government didn't number patents. After a fire destroyed the patent house that year, it assigned numbers to all patents registered between 1793 and 1836. These are known as the "X" patents. Jennings's patent papers were never recovered after the fire, and it was recorded as patent 3306X.

Patent number 3306X was also important because it recognized Jennings as a free US citizen. Strong forces such as the American Colonization Society opposed and disputed the right of free people of African descent even to be American citizens.

Just the notion of an inventor of color was contrary to the squirrelly science of racial inferiority that was popular at the time. But that didn't stop Jennings from doing what he knew every American citizen had the right to do—file a patent under his name. That was not the case for Henry Boyd, a Kentuckian born into slavery who purchased his freedom. Fearful that racism would prevent him from patenting his corded "Boyd Bedstead" invention, Boyd partnered with a white carpenter, allowing him to receive the patent.

Despite all the limitations put upon them, slaves also did their share of inventing, for which their owners wanted compensation. Slaveholder Oscar Stewart tried to patent a "cotton scraper" invented by a slave known only as Ned. "When did a free Negro ever invent anything," he cried on a banner, as if he had accomplished something. Denied his patent application, Stewart sold the product without it. Benjamin Montgomery was enslaved in Virginia, where he invented a steam-driven propeller to replace clunky riverboat paddlewheels. His owner happened to be Jefferson Davis's brother. He too tried to cash in on enslaved ingenuity.

The concept behind the rejections was as simple as it was wrongheaded in many ways: Property couldn't own property. With that philosophy, slave-submitted patents were rejected. In 1857, the US government finally ruled that inventions by slaves couldn't be patented. Confederate president Jefferson Davis made sure the patent law was changed in his new government. Jennings was lucky only because he was born free and his patent was protected by the fact that he was legally a US citizen.

Jennings's patent brought him and his family wealth and worry. The competition was fierce. One rival who threatened Jennings's business was

Abraham Cox. A black tailor with white financial backing, he tried to steal Jennings's new cleaning process. In newspaper ads placed in the *New York Gazette* in 1820, Cox made claims to a "New Discovery" that saved garments "by repairing, scouring, hot sponging and cleaning." Jennings confronted his rival by moving his store to 64 Nassau Street—right next to Cox, Gilbert & Company.

Cox didn't take the news of Jennings's patent or new location very well. He damaged his neighbor's business. Oil of vitriol (acid) was splattered across an engraved glass sign on Jennings's storefront. Cox tore down posters from around the city that advertised Jennings's invention while continuing to run his misleading ads. According to the December 7, 1821, edition of the *New York American*, to avoid suspicion of vandalism, Cox slightly damaged his own shop. He then offered a reward for the culprit.

Displaying an ability that would serve his family well, Jennings brought a lawsuit against Cox. The trial began on November 29, 1821, in the Marine Court (the city's court of record). Covered by the press, the case revealed Jennings's views on wealth. It's clear that he didn't approve of Cox's rich lifestyle. He called Cox a "first rate dandy" and a man who "cuts considerable dash in his mode of living."

Unlike the reserved Jennings, Cox pranced around the city in a "horse and gig" for the "purpose of monopolizing this profitable business." The key piece of evidence was the "Letters of Patent" signed by John Quincy Adams.[1] It bore the gold seal of the US government. After a half hour the white jury agreed with Jennings. He was awarded fifty dollars in damages.

Although Elizabeth wasn't born yet, this family episode must have been retold many times and taught her to stand up for her beliefs. In those days a patent was protected for fourteen years. In 1836, patent laws were revised to give a seven-year extension to certain inventions. Today, a patent lasts for twenty years. With the rights to his invention established, Jennings used his income to focus on improving life for the black community. In his 1855 autobiography, *A Fugitive Negro*, Samuel Ringgold Ward recalled working for Jennings as a sixteen-year-old clerk. Ward said he was "one of the most worthy of the coloured race." Ward went on to become a well-known abolitionist and newspaper reporter.

Jennings was a founding member of many early civil rights groups. Among them were the Wilberforce Society, the New York African Society for Mutual Relief, and the Phoenix Society. Later on, he formed the New York Vigilance Committee and the Legal Rights Association. He was also a key member of the first three National Conventions of Free People of Colour and a trustee of the Abyssinian Baptist Church.

Emancipation Day, July 4, 1827, became a holiday to celebrate the end of slavery in New York. According to a retrospective on the event printed in the *Frederick Douglass' Paper* in 1855, displays of appreciation were held throughout the state with the primary services held in Albany, Rochester, and Manhattan.

> *In New York City an overwhelming meeting was addressed in eloquent terms by Mr. Thomas L. Jennings: and the meeting was graced and ennobled by the presence of ex-Governor Daniel D. Tompkins,*[2] *the author of the Emancipation act.*

The white press in Manhattan remained unimpressed. While several papers put Emancipation on its front pages, the news was brief and buried below the fold several days after the event. Under the subheading "Commemoration by Africans," the *New York Daily Advertiser* said the day was "celebrated by the class of inhabitants most interested in the event in an appropriate and highly becoming manner." Some showed their thinly veiled prejudices between the lines. The *American* added, "The music was unusually good; . . . as will be readily believed from the acknowledged talent for music of the African race."

The Fourth of July would remain a flashpoint for violence during the existence of slavery. It was a trigger to unleash white mobs against black citizens on more than one occasion throughout the country. African Americans were well aware of the irony of the celebration and looked upon it sarcastically at times, as this song parody of the recently written "My Country, 'Tis of Thee" taken from the July 27, 1838, edition of the *Colored American* shows.

My country! 'tis for thee,
Dark land of slavery,
For Thee I weep;
Land where the slave has signed,
Land, where he toiled and died,
To serve a tyrant's pride—
For thee I weep,

My native country! thee,
Land of the noble free—
Of Liberty—
My native country, weep;
A fast in sorrow keep,
The stain is foul and deep
Of slavery.

When Jubilation Day (the first anniversary of Emancipation in New York) came, it was celebrated on July 5, 1828. That day, the city was alive with anticipation. However, some bystanders had nefarious deeds in mind. The sudden blare of horns hushed the murmuring crowd and seemed to lift the gray veil of clouds that draped over the rooftops of the old city. In the full sunlight the magnificent colors of the gathering parade stood in sharp contrast to the drab, muddy streets of lower Manhattan. Thousands of African American men and boys milled about waiting for the procession to begin.

Jennings was among those marking the first anniversary of the end of slavery. Marchers lined up under the coat of arms of their group, trade, or organization. Because he was a member of so many charitable associations, some of his friends might have asked with a grin which banner Jennings would strut under. Perhaps others remembering the moving speech he gave at the New York State Emancipation celebration the year before hoped he might deliver another one.

First in line was the New York African Society for Mutual Relief, which Jennings helped establish in 1808. It stayed in existence until 1945. They were followed by the Wilberforce Benevolent Society and the Clarkson Benevolent Society. Each group had a band and slogans of civic pride hoisted on standards high above the crowd. The oldest Am I not a Man and a Brother? banner that Jennings carried in his youth was still used. The Wilberforce Society held aloft a powder-blue treasure chest and gold key bearing its collected funds as a show of economic strength. Street dancers, magicians, jugglers, and "walking" statues were all part of the moving festivities.

Samuel Hardenburgh, the grand marshal, arrived decked out in a black tricornered hat, scarlet long-coat, and yellow buckskin pants mounted on a magnificent white horse. When he drew his sword high overhead, rifles fired a salute signaling the procession's start. Lined up five across, the estimated four thousand marchers began their trek up from the Battery shoreline on Broadway toward Orange Street. The joyous chants and cheers of onlookers echoed down the narrow cobbled and oyster-shelled lanes. Wearing gold-embroidered red, green, and purple bandannas, West Indians strode in a continuous dance step to the beat of Guinea drums, tin whistles, and banjos. Others wore old uniforms to honor relatives who served in the American Revolution and War of 1812.

The majesty and power of the day was a point of pride for the black community, but everyone didn't feel the love. One newspaper reported that a white grocer pulled his horse-drawn wagon into the street trying to stop the parade's progress. Other whites threw things and staged mock ceremonies along the route to belittle the event. But the marchers kept coming. Onlookers described the incident as an advancing wall of black males that "brushed aside the impediments and obstacles placed in front of them" and proceeded undeterred.

There were others among the spectators and marchers that day equally impressed by this display of solidarity. One was an escaped teenaged slave descended from an African warrior prince named Henry Highland Garnet. He became a fiery abolitionist preaching armed rebellion by slaves. The other was a young white boy born on Pearl Street near the parade route. African culture, music, and the diversity he was exposed to as a child in Manhattan profoundly influenced Herman Melville's writing.

Many of the city's African American leaders believed their culture now needed its own voice. That year, around the time Elizabeth, the youngest of the Jennings children, was born, Thomas Jennings was among the backers who helped form *Freedom's Journal* as the nation's first black newspaper.

"We wish to plead our own cause," stated coeditors John Russwurm and Samuel E. Cornish in the first issue. "Too long have others spoken for us."

The paper filled a void at a critical time in black history. *Freedom's Journal* was a four-page weekly paper that grew to become the publication of record for African Americans. It featured poetry and articles on literature, history, and important events. Its subscription base reached eleven states, Canada, Europe, and Haiti. The *Journal* also provided Jennings's and other black-run businesses with advertising space. Marriages, deaths, and other news was available for three dollars a year.

During the 1830s, Elizabeth's brothers moved to Boston to make their way in the world. William had his father's knack for business. He quickly became a successful clothing dealer. He had a sharp wit and generous nature. William once used his own money to print five hundred flyers to promote the black newspaper the *Weekly Advocate*. He also purchased twenty subscriptions to help get it started in New England.

William and Thomas Jr.'s savvy business sense also brought something unexpected. One night in 1837, their store was broken into from the back cellar. Clothing, jewelry, and watches amounting to four hundred dollars were stolen. Within months of the break-in, William sold the clothing business and started another. The *Liberator* announced that Jennings's sons had "removed" to a spacious building at 100 Court Street. Located next to a factory, they opened a curiosity shop full of "fancy articles—watches, swords, and pistols . . . surgical, nautical and musical instruments." The young men paid "a liberal price for any ornaments or curiosities."

By all accounts, William was "unassuming and beloved by all who knew him." He quickly rose to become vice president of the prestigious Adelphic Union Library Association. There William and Thomas became fast friends with the abolitionist and journalist William C. Nell. Dedicated to "the literary improvement of its members," the group featured speakers such as Horace Mann, Charles Sumner, and William Lloyd Garrison. William had a sharp wit as well. Describing the lack of meeting space available for blacks in Boston, he wrote in the *Weekly Advocate*:

> *Fancy one thousand persons, (freemen of New England) crammed in a horse stable, proclaiming liberty, while old Faneuil Hall, the reputed*

cradle of Liberty, which rocks any cause but Anti-Slavery, was fast barred against them.

At a time when African Americans weren't allowed to enroll in white medical schools, Thomas Jennings Jr. chose to become a dentist. Formal dental schools began to appear in the 1840s but were not open to black students until after the Civil War. Thomas was perhaps among the first apprenticed African Americans to perform dental surgery. For a brief time in the late 1840s, he practiced dentistry at 185 Broadway in Rochester, New York. Eventually Dr. Jennings moved his practice to New Orleans, Louisiana. There he was among the city's wealthiest landowners and the chief vestryman for St. Thomas Episcopal Church. His financial acumen prevented the parish from going under. It still exists today.

In Boston, Thomas studied for three years under Dr. Daniel Mann, a respected dental surgeon and abolitionist. Jennings was adept at the new methods of forming artificial teeth, filling cavities with lithodeon, and making dentures. A tribute to Thomas's skill was published in the June 11, 1840, issue of the *Liberator*. In a letter to the editor, the writer "A.C." states, "Mr. J., by his attention, industry and native ingenuity, has made himself skillful in his profession . . . [he] is well worthy of [our] patronage."

His travels with Dr. Mann and others to medical lectures and abolitionist meetings also had an unintended purpose—exposing Boston's segregated public transportation practices. At least three instances involving Thomas Jennings Jr. were reported in newspapers. The first occurred in Charlestown on June 16, 1840, as reported in a letter to the editor of the *Liberator* by F.F. Manford. A white man riding on a horse-drawn bus, Manford was outraged when the conductor grabbed Jennings from behind, preventing him from sitting down. In protest, Manford left his seat, causing a scuffle on the street that was broken up by the police.

The following year, while returning from Salem to Boston on the Eastern Railroad with Dr. Mann, Thomas was ordered out of the first-class compartment he paid for along with his white companions. After they refused to leave, railroad workers forcibly removed them from the train.

The last incident occurred on Saturday, October 21, 1841, when Dr. Jennings was returning to Boston from New Bedford when he spotted two white associates who invited him to sit with them. After several stops the conductor demanded the doctor leave for the "Jim Crow" car and that he leave his white contemporaries behind. Jennings refused to go, leading to a confrontation between railway workers and the three men. Eventually Dr. Jennings left the car, but "the conductor and another man still handled him roughly," wrote H. Cummings to the *Liberator*, "throwing him upon the platform outside, striking him, and otherwise bruising him."

With the public agitated and these transit incidents increasing, Dr. Mann brought a lawsuit against the Eastern Railroad and conductor George Harrington for assault and battery against an unnamed black man. On Saturday, October 30, 1841, Judge Simmons of the Police Court heard Mann's case. His lawyer claimed the railroad had "no legal right to separate passengers on the basis of color." The case caused quite a stir in Boston, but in the end the judge sided with the railroad. He stated that the conductor's actions were justified because of "the disorderly and unlawful conduct of Dr. Mann and his friends."

The verdict piqued Bostonians who smugly believed their city was the "Athens of America" and a shining example of freedom to the world. At a December 1841 meeting led by Frederick Douglass and Abby Kelley, the Boston anti-slavery society resolved to confront the segregation that Thomas Jennings Jr. faced through peaceful protest. Thanks in large part to the efforts of this group, in 1843, the Commonwealth of Massachusetts passed a law that "No rail corporation shall . . . give a preference in accommodation to any one or more persons over other, on account of descent, sect, or color."

The lessons of Mann's lost transit case in 1841 stuck with teenaged Elizabeth and her father back in New York. The Police Court in Boston was for criminal cases, not civil rights cases. Besides, New York was the Empire City, and when you win there, you win on the big stage. Likewise, if you lose, everyone sees you go down in flames. Their test, their trial, would not come for another fourteen years.

In the meantime, the Jennings family soldiered on. Elizabeth and her sisters followed their mother's example as well. They contributed their skills to numerous activist causes. Matilda was recognized as one of Manhattan's top dressmakers and worked for many charitable groups. Years later, Sarah ran an exclusive boarding house supporting San Francisco's growing African American artistic community. Elizabeth was among the first wave of black women choosing education as a career path.

Even though the Jennings family dedicated themselves to social causes, they lived in the business world. Each member knew what it took to be successful. Like the stitches in a garment, the Jenningses held together any cause they supported. They were the secretaries, administrators, and dues collectors behind the scenes. Without them, the stirring speeches and social progress would never have happened. Little did the family know that in the years ahead their "good old New York stock" would yield such an abundance of timber from its youngest sapling.

Chapter II

The Wizard of Whipple City

The noblest forms of manhood are seldom cradled in luxury.

—Rev. Robert Stuart MacArthur,
Psi Upsilon Memorial Service for President Arthur

To describe the Arthurs as dirt-poor would be considered an understatement by anyone who met them. Poverty defined the family as much as any coat of arms did the lineage of their Scottish ancestors—hardly the stuff that made future presidents, or so it would seem.

The Arthurs could trace their roots back to the fifteenth-century Clan Campbell as the MacArthurs. Eventually the "Mac" was dropped from the name. In the early eighteenth century, Jane Campbell moved from Scotland to Ulster to marry Gavin Arthur. They had a son, Alán. One thing the Arthurs were good at was producing male heirs. In 1796, Chester's father, William, was born to Alán and Eliza McHarg in Dreen, Ireland. When he was a youngster, a stone wall crumpled on his leg, giving the boy a decided limp.

Since he was unable to perform basic farming chores, the family scrimped together enough money to educate William in hopes he could have a career as a teacher. He graduated from Belfast College with a classical education. Unrest in Ulster and an unstable economy in Ireland convinced the young educator to emigrate to Quebec. After spending some time there, he took a position just fifteen miles from the Vermont border with the Free School of Royal Foundation in Dunham, Quebec. This also put William near the household of the Stones, who would later become part of his family.

During the 1750s, Uriah Stone, the family's patriarch, became a major during the Seven Years' War, also known as the French and Indian War.

Uriah reenlisted with the New Hampshire and Vermont militias as a corporal during the American Revolution, naming one of his five sons George Washington Stone. In all, he had thirteen children, started a tannery, and operated a ferry used to cross the Connecticut River.

At the turn of the nineteenth century, George Stone and his four brothers relocated to Berkshire, Vermont, where he married Judith Stevens, who may have been part Native American. They had two sons and a daughter, Malvina, together. At age eighteen, Malvina met a sharp-tongued, ambitious schoolteacher some six years older than herself. Within a year, William Arthur and Malvina eloped.

The Arthur Clan in America had begun.

It seemed that every time the Arthurs moved another child arrived. The Arthurs had nine, all but one living into adulthood, according to the Arthur family Bible. In 1822, Regina, the first, arrived while the family still lived in Dunham. By the time Jane arrived in 1824, William had moved his brood across the border into Vermont. With the Erie Canal nearing completion, Burlington was a burgeoning port town on Lake Champlain. It was the perfect place for William to study law at the offices of Vermont governor Cornelius Van Ness while teaching during the day. A move to Jericho, Vermont, in 1825 brought along another daughter, Almeda. William began to wonder if he would ever have a son to continue his name and legacy. Nevertheless, William continued to pursue his goal of becoming a lawyer as his growing family moved north in 1827 to Waterville, Vermont. The Arthurs rang in 1828 with the birth of their fourth daughter, Ann Eliza.

Other movements were afoot as well. In the early nineteenth century, the New England region was undergoing a "Second Great Awakening" of religious fervor. It was in response to scientific discoveries and the rationalism that spurred the American and French Revolutions in the past century. Revival meetings that jolted spirituality back into the lives of everyday Americans were taking place all across New England. William Arthur attended one such meeting sponsored by the Free Will Baptists in Burlington. During it, a lightning bolt of devotion struck him.

William Arthur felt he was being called to the ministry. He quickly gave up his legal career and Presbyterianism for a Baptist preacher's frock. Soon William was licensed to preach, and in the spring of 1828, he was ordained. Once again, the Arthur family found itself on the move, this time to a picturesque farming community folded into the Green Mountains.

Established in 1763 near the Canadian border, North Fairfield was filled with green pastures and rolling hills that must have reminded William Arthur of his boyhood in Ireland. However, the home they came to live in was nothing like the charming rustic New England farmhouses seen in lithographs.

It was a small, dank log cabin as they waited for a new parsonage to be built. With fewer than fifty members, the North Fairfield congregation wasn't wealthy. Arthur was paid only two hundred fifty dollars annually, which meant he had to teach and preach in other towns in Vermont and Canada to earn a living. It was hard to keep the new minister's large family fed during these harsh mountain winters. His wife was expecting their fifth child, and the Elder Arthur, as he was now called in an acknowledgment to his staunch devotion to the cloth, groused to visitors and friends about the meager pickings of food and firewood his family had to survive upon.

As summer faded into the fall of 1829, the Elder Arthur fully expected another girl. When the time came, they sent for Dr. Chester Abell, a friend and relative of the Stone family. One can imagine William fuddling about the musty room reading and thinking of girl's names as his wife went into labor once again. To be sure, they would name this one Malvina after her. As time passed, he might have dozed off in one of the few chairs the family owned, only to be awakened by the nurse announcing that the Arthurs now had a son.

By all accounts, William hardly believed the nurse's words. Usually a sour and serious man, William spontaneously jumped in the air with delight and submitted for a moment to the "wiles of the Old Serpent." Despite his lame leg, he danced an Irish jig throughout their cabin home. It was a demonstration of frivolity he would have admonished his parishioners for showing. William immediately named the boy Chester in gratitude to the family doctor who delivered him and added the middle name of Alán to honor his father.

It was October 5, 1829, the day Chester Alán Arthur's name was added to the family Bible, and neighbors still remembered the minister's dance decades later.

Nearly two years earlier, some 350 miles south in New York City, the fifth and youngest child, Elizabeth, was born into the Jennings family.

With a son now in tow whom he could mold in his image, the Elder Arthur turned his energies toward more worldly concerns. According to Thomas Reeves in *Gentleman Boss*, William began attending anti-slavery meetings at the behest of the Reverend Orson S. Murray. Like William, Murray also felt a calling to the Baptist ministry, but his life changed a second time in 1832 when he began reading William Lloyd Garrison's abolitionist newspaper, the *Liberator*, along with his treatise *Thoughts on African Colonization.* He then joined the growing abolitionist movement. Murray, in turn, converted the Elder Arthur to abolitionism. William began to meet and hear important people in the anti-slavery movement such as Gerrit Smith, Spencer Kellogg, and David Ruggles.

The cause wasn't a popular one in Vermont during the 1830s, especially in the Green Mountain region. It was an odd dichotomy for the first state to outlaw slavery, in 1777, to show such ambivalence toward the abolitionist movement. In *Vermont Attitudes toward Slavery: The Need for a Closer Look*, J. Kevin Graffagnino argues that "a segment of Vermont's population in the first half of the nineteenth century at least tolerated, if not supported, slavery."

In a letter from 1837, Charles B. Fletcher describes a trip to South Carolina with his father, Isaac Fletcher of Lyndon, Vermont.

> *They [slaves] are much better off than the abolitionists are generally willing to allow. I have not seen any of them skinned, roasted and devoured since I have been here. They are well fed, well clothed, well housed and not one half of the work is exacted from them that is exacted from our farmers from his men . . . They are the happiest race of mortals I have ever saw. Any person who abuses his slaves here is looked upon in the same light as a man who abuses his family among us.*

Nearly 500 miles from the Mason-Dixon Line, the argument against slavery in rural New England was intellectual, not visceral. Abolitionists wouldn't get much sympathy or support from people who felt they worked harder than slaves. At least 124 anti-slavery organizations existed in the North by 1835. As their numbers grew, so did the opposition, particularly along the New York/Vermont corridor, where the Underground Railroad to Canada was strong.

The Elder Arthur was woefully overqualified for his teaching and ministerial positions in these small towns. Besides his degree in the classics from Belfast College, he was fluent in Greek, Latin, and Hebrew—not exactly a skill set these hardscrabble farmers would hold in high esteem or put at the top of their lists for success.

His railing against slavery in North Fairfield cost him parishioners, donations, and needed supplies, but the Elder Arthur was steadfast in his allegiance to the cause, as Murray pointed out years later.

> *He clung to his pulpit and preached the doctrines of Christianity but was ever ready to extend the right hand of fellowship to me and, for that matter, any other anti-slavery lecturer in the country.*

Likewise, the Elder Arthur's instructional style could be described at best as "tough love." If he felt parishioners were dozing off in church or students weren't paying attention in class, he would interrupt the proceedings to call each of them out. He had a thick Irish brogue to go along with a razor-sharp wit that he used to cut opponents to ribbons. William's students lived in constant fear of his volcanic temper. He had the unwavering glare of a bird of prey sizing up its next meal. Caught in that penetrating gaze, said one former Arthur pupil, "the best thing a malcontent could do was maintain an armed neutrality while Mr. Arthur was head of affairs."

When times were particularly tough, the Arthurs took in student boarders that the Elder Arthur tutored. A surviving student recalled, "Instead of my attending school I recited to Elder Arthur . . . He maintained the most rigid government in his family . . . and was earnest and enthusiastic in preaching his doctrines." The Elder Arthur often joked that if not for his bum leg he could chase down the wayward acolytes in his care and bring them to justice. Even with these abrasive ways, the pastor was still a charismatic and persuasive orator. His sermons could go on for hours as he kept his parishioners mesmerized with his words.

He [Elder Arthur] drew audiences unheard of before in that rustic community [North Fairfield]. He at first preached in the district schoolhouse, which soon failed to hold half his audience. Finally, a spacious neighboring barn was pressed into service as a place of worship.

Ensconced in their newly built home in North Fairfield, the Arthurs brought their fifth daughter, Malvina Almeda, into the world during the spring of 1832. Eventually Elder Arthur's resolute abolitionism wore down the faithful. His message grated on church leaders, he began losing his flock, and it was time to move on again.

During 1834, the Arthurs relocated south to Hinesburg, Vermont. Their second son, William, was born in that quaint Champlain Valley village not far from Burlington. Two years later, George was born in Perry, New York, a hamlet forty miles south of Rochester. He died at age two. Mary, the ninth and last child to join the family, was born in July 1841. The joy of her birth was tempered with the loss of eighteen-year-old Jane in April 1842. She was buried in the newly opened section of the Albany Rural Cemetery in Menands, New York. Just as Cypress Hills Cemetery in Brooklyn, New York, became the resting place for the Jennings family, the Albany Rural Cemetery became the final repose for the Arthur Clan.

By 1839, the Arthur family had settled in Union Village, not far from Saratoga in upstate New York. Back then many people still used the town's original name—Whipple City. Today, it's called Greenwich. The only location that still echoes that name is an abandoned eatery on Route 29 in Greenwich, once home to the Original Whipple City Pizza and the Whipple Burger.

The first designation came from one of the town's earliest entrepreneurs, Job Whipple, who settled there in the early 1760s and started a successful cotton mill, among other businesses. The community was planted near the Hudson River, the blue ribbon of the Battenkill gently wrapped around it as if it were a present.

The many lakes, streams, and waterfalls made Whipple City ideal for water-powered grist, lumber, and paper mills. It also made it easy to slip into nearby Canada undetected. The village was proud of its many "factories" making wool, flax, and land plaster. Unlike today's factories, most

First known as Whipple City, the town grew into Union Village and eventually Greenwich, New York, after the Civil War. COURTESY GREENWICH HISTORICAL SOCIETY

of these operations only employed small numbers of people. The area also boasted rich freshwater fishing and game reserves. Perhaps it was here that ten-year-old Chester first developed his lifelong love of sport fishing.

For the Elder Arthur, ministering for the Bottskill Baptist Church in Whipple City brought him a step closer to the big leagues. His salary swelled to a hefty five hundred dollars a year, finally providing the financial stability his family needed. More importantly, kindred spirits and men of his own ilk lived in Union Village. Among them was Dr. Hiram Corliss, one of the first abolitionists in the state, who, along with lawyer Leonard Gibbs, operated a branch of the Underground Railroad as an alternative to the main Syracuse and Central New York corridor to Canada. Dr. Corliss also converted a previous elder of the Bottskill Baptist church, Nathaniel Cover, to abolitionism. Surely Corliss, though his friendship with Gerrit Smith, heard of the bombastic Elder Arthur's aptitude for hurling abolitionist lightning bolts from the pulpit and welcomed his presence.

The movement attracted a determined young lawyer with political aspirations from Union Village, New York. Erastus Dean Culver was an abolitionist in the area. At an early age he was driven to become a pivotal figure in New York state's abolitionist movement by his mother's dying words: "My son, I am looking at you for the last time . . . Stand for the right. Plead for the poor and oppressed." Later in his life as a political leader, spokesman, and civil rights attorney, he had no rivals. At an 1840 debate in Albany, New York, it was reported that Culver lured away Daniel Webster supporters "by the charm of his eloquence."

But in 1834, more often than not, Culver was on the run, keeping a step ahead of pro-slavery mobs. In one such case, a meeting at the Dutch Reformed Church in Argyle, New York, was delayed by pro-slavery forces locking the church doors with iron bars and nailing the windows shut. Undeterred, Culver and the others climbed into the church through a small window and held their meeting. Throughout the event twenty armed men harassed the group, threatening to beat them while racing a wagon around the building with a hanged scarecrow made to look like a black man. A sign with the words Judge Lynch was nailed to its chest.

Culver reported the incident in an article he wrote for the *Vermont Tribune* and ended it with this prediction about slavery: "Jehovah has decreed it. The frowning tyrant to the South, his cringing echo at the North, the cowardly minister, the fawning politician, and the mob-encouraging press, are preparing for the condemnation that awaits them."

Word spreads quickly in a small town like Union, and when Erastus Culver heard of the Elder Arthur, it was not long before he was attending the Elder Arthur's sermons. He struck up a friendship with the firebrand abolitionist preacher, who showed no fear in voicing his convictions. Culver also took notice of the minister's bright young son "Chet." He would be one of the most important people Chester met during his life. The youngster was anxious to please his demanding father. His homeschooling in the classics showed Culver that this boy wasn't destined to become another millworker or farmhand in Whipple City.

Young Chester's future destiny wasn't on his mind as he explored the natural wonders of the area and played games with his chums. One can imagine him seeking friends on a break from the intense fire of his father's pent-up knowledge to roll rusty barrel hoops with a stick down Park Street, where the Bottskill Baptist Church sat overlooking the Battenkill River. It was easy to pull jacks from your pocket and play knucklebones on an old stump or toss your pocketknife into the ground and play mumblety-peg. All chuck-farthing called for was a few buttons or stones that could be tossed in a cup.

Chester's fraternity brother R.S. MacArthur once described the Elder Arthur in the following way: "There was in him much both of the lion and of the lamb."

But his family didn't see it that way. The ferociousness of the lion overwhelmed all other actions. In a series of articles for the Vermont Historical Society based on the Arthur family papers, Reeves points out that well into adulthood the family was terrorized by the Elder Arthur. Unquestionably, Chester had his father's ear, causing his sisters and brother to turn to him for solace and protection. He could bear the intensity of his father's intellect and play Aesop's Androcles to his father's lion. Circumstance, a terrible temper, and physical limitations robbed the Elder Arthur of the career he wanted. His first son would pull that thorn out of his hand and become the crusading lawyer his father never became.

Much like a wizard studying alchemy at a young age, Chester learned to tame his lion father, not with force but by using the magic of empathy, sincerity, and compromise. This was evident in an oft-cited anecdote that demonstrates his leadership. As with any story brought to light after someone reaches fame, be wary. However, the preponderance of these accounts reveals the youngster's developing personality and an ability to rally resources.

According to the *New York Evening Post,* many years later a Whipple City lad recalled Chet's organizing skills.

> *When Chester was a boy, you might see him in the village street after a shower, watching boys building a mud dam across the rivulet in the roadway. Pretty soon he would be ordering this one to bring stones, another sticks, and others sods and mud to finish the dam; and they would all do his bidding without question. But he took good care not to get any of the dirt on his hands.*

The dirt would come much later on and in a different venue. For now, Chet was getting ready to attend his first public school. He had outgrown his father's lesson plans and needed to develop an academic record that would allow him to continue his studies in college. In the fall he would attend school at Mrs. Wait's house on Bleecker Street in Union Village. Around the same time, less than a half mile away on Gray Avenue, a nineteen-year-old schoolteacher taught classes at Fairbanks Cottage.

Susan B. Anthony and Chester A. Arthur never crossed paths in old Whipple City, but they were destined to forty years later in the White House under more tense conditions. Neither one was aware of how close they might have come to forming a student-teacher relationship years before. At the same time, in Manhattan, another fledgling teacher was told African American women weren't suited to be classroom instructors. Elizabeth Jennings would have an uphill battle to participate in her chosen field.

In the classroom and amongst his peers, Chet's personality began to solidify. James I. Lowrie, who ran the Union Village school, described Chet as "frank and open in manners and genteel in disposition." The Arthur family had a good run in Whipple City; as the *History of Baptists in Vermont* reported, the Elder Arthur "remained for about five years enjoying a peaceful and prosperous pastorate."

Homeschooled, Chester entered the academy in Union Village to build an academic record for college. COURTESY GREENWICH HISTORICAL SOCIETY

In August 1843, the Elder Arthur became a naturalized US citizen. The following year, Chet was accepted to the Lyceum and Academy in Schenectady, New York. The Arthurs were once again on the move. The same issues and conflicts that dogged the country dogged the Arthur family too. Education could be a bridge to a better understanding between warring familial factions, but in this case, it widened the gap.

Chapter III

Slavery in the Empire City

Was there ever such a sunny street as this Broadway!

—Charles Dickens,
American Notes

By the mid-nineteenth century, New York was a city in search of itself. It was as much a cow town as it was a bulging metropolis. In many ways it was a city as hard as the granite bedrock that would make it an ideal foundation for the skyscrapers and commerce of future generations.

Broadway was the main artery of the city. It began as a Native American pathway for the Lenape people called the Wickquasgeck Trail that followed the length of the thirteen-mile island. During Dutch colonial times, this road passed by the fort of New Amsterdam. It was called *Breede weg* by the Dutch, which the British later translated to "Broadway." In the seventeenth century, it extended as far north as the Wall Street commons, and by Elizabeth Jennings's time, the avenue reached Forty-Second Street and Longacre Square, now called Times Square.

Taking a short walk up Broadway on the cobbled roads Jennings traveled every day, a passerby saw a crosscut of city life. Not far from her home, flags of the world and wild exhibits drew 400,000 visitors a year to P.T. Barnum's American Museum on Ann Street. People marveled at displays from around the world. Little person General Tom Thumb and conjoined twins Chang and Eng performed daily. Children chased Barnum's bulletin wagon as it wobbled through the streets slapping exhibit posters on buildings.

Nearby, the infamous Five Points loomed. "I would rather risk myself in an Indian fight," wrote Davy Crockett in his 1835 memoir upon encountering the area for the first time, "than venture among these creatures after night." The five-story Old Brewery building was still an imposing structure at the mouth of the intersection of streets that slithered and coiled snakelike through the Points. The school Elizabeth attended as a girl was on Mulberry Street along the infamous Bend. Across the way was the dangerous Bottle Alley; behind it, Bandit's Roost.

Make a wrong turn and end up on Elm Street (Lafayette/Elk Streets today). Elm was a long, slobbering wet kiss of a road gurgling with all the ooze and ills that the nearly twenty-year-old Tombs prison brought with it. Nightly the Black Maria prison wagon, with no windows or means of escape, sped by. The echoing screams of the women inside the wagon could stop a heart.

Author William M. Bobo put it more viscerally in 1852 when he published *Glimpses of New York City*, comparing Manhattan to human anatomy, "City Hall being the heart, the Tombs the stomach, the Five Points the bowels, the Parks the lungs, Broadway the nose, the Piers the feet."

It's hard to imagine today, but two streams once intersected near Broadway that required bridges to cross. One was the Stone Bridge at Canal Street; the other was called the Kissing Bridge near the junction where Chatham met Roosevelt Street. Custom allowed the collector (assumed male) to exact a toll in the form of a kiss from his female companion (no shunpiking allowed). Sixteen soggy acres near Maiden Lane and William Street was known from the old Dutch days as the Shoemaker's Pasture. In the summer, people would travel uptown to the Petersfield Farm or pick blackberries along the road in nearby Bowery Village. Others shucked oysters from the plentiful beds surrounding the island or sold hot corn on the streets to bring in extra money. Children would sneak over to the Screw Dock on South Street to watch two-hundred-ton ships hoisted out of the water for repairs.

The majestic Astor House Hotel stood on Barclay Street. This five-story Greek Revival building had 309 rooms with gaslights and seventeen bathrooms. Among its guests were former president Andrew Jackson, Davy Crockett, and British author Charles Dickens.

Further uptown under Bleecker Street, the basement vault of Pfaff's Beer Hall played host to various aspiring writers, ne'er-do-wells, and actors led by newspaperman Walt Whitman. In this dim, smoke-filled cave, the bohemians recalled that the late Edgar Allan Poe rented a room in Patrick Brennan's farmhouse at Eighty-Fourth and Broadway, where he wrote "The Balloon Hoax" for the ***Sun*** and "The Raven" as well.

If Poe had lingered in the Empire City longer, he would have witnessed one of the more bizarre events in its history. Emulating Saint Patrick, in the summer of 1849, the police drove the wild hogs roaming the city streets out of lower Manhattan.[3] What could Poe's grim imagination have come up with staring out his bedroom window as some six thousand pigs were banished beyond the city's northern limits? That summer, hog drives herded twenty thousand swine off city streets, according to Burrows and Wallace. That didn't deter the faithful at Pfaff's. They still read Poe's works aloud while patrons drank German beer and ate cheese and free-range pork sausages. They were the Beat Generation one hundred years before its time.

Visitors approaching Bond Street were in awe of Tripler's Hall. The city's new 5,500-seat opera house was billed as one of the largest music halls in the world. Locals would tell stories of how the hall was built for the "Swedish Nightingale," Jenny Lind. She performed for a whopping three dollars a seat. Former slave Elizabeth Taylor Greenfield, known as the "Black Swan," returning from a concert before England's Queen Victoria, sang there too.

For African American patrons looking to purchase a ticket to see Elizabeth Taylor Greenfield on stage, they would be disappointed. As Frederick Douglass noted in his newspaper in 1853, on each concert placard this message appeared: "Particular Notice—No colored person can be admitted, as there is no part of the house appropriated for them."

Known as the "black codes," these laws were intended to keep slaves from revolting. Each state had its own set that dictated how free African Americans were to be treated socially as well. Although New York had been a Free State since 1827, its black citizens were restricted in voting, excluded as jurors, and denied access to higher education. Black New Yorkers also were limited as to where they could live or where they could attend church or other social events. If a white person objected to an African American riding public transit, the black person was forcibly removed.

Except on special occasions, Barnum's Museum barred African Americans from its doors. The Astor House would welcome blacks as porters, bellhops, and cooks, but not as guests. Pfaffians allowed women (albeit via a separate door), but welcoming black patrons wasn't on the table. Chided by Frederick Douglass for playing before segregated audiences, Greenfield eventually performed several benefit concerts open to African Americans.

To help create more opportunities for blacks, Thomas Jennings pushed to create the Phoenix Society. Its purpose was "to promote the improvement of the coloured people in morals, literature, and the mechanical arts." One of the society's more important contributions was a census of all African Americans in Manhattan to determine who could read and write. Jennings was its second vice president and surveyed the Fourteenth District of the city. The society also built a large cultural center with a library.

Slavery for centuries before Thomas Jennings had cast a long and hideous shadow across Manhattan, starting as early as the 1600s. It infected every aspect of society. Slavery started in New York when the Dutch West India Company sought to tap into America's natural resources including timber, furs, and waterways. The company underestimated how difficult those riches would be to extract. Few whites were willing to work the hard, rocky soil and marshlands of lower Manhattan. Early plans to dig a network of canals similar to Holland's were quickly abandoned.

Bonded Africans were among the first settlers in the Dutch colony. They arrived in 1626 when the West India Company consigned eleven purchased African men known as Atlantic Creoles to New Amsterdam. Dutch and Spanish custom gave slaves a Christian first name with the last name identifying their place of origin. Among that first group of slaves were Paulo D'Angola, Simon Congo, and Peter Santomee. Slaves cut timber, harvested grain, and built roads while performing many other skilled tasks.

By the 1630s, land grants with the promise of "company negros" to work the fields were hawked as incentives to lure settlers. A European laborer cost 280 Dutch guilders a year, plus food and lodging, while 300 guilders purchased an African slave. Slavery was already the economic engine driving growth in the New World. This new stream of skilled and enforced labor helped turn a struggling trading post into the thriving community of New Amsterdam.

During the early days of the Dutch colony, the legal bounds of slavery were not well defined. Because of religious practices, the Dutch rarely referred to the African population as slaves. To them, slavery was more an assignment of labor than a mark of social status or a cultural stigma that needed cruel laws to enforce. Under Dutch law, a slave was allowed to testify against a white person. New Amsterdam blacks expected equal treatment. In 1634, five slaves traveled to Holland to sue for back wages, claiming they should receive the same pay as white servants. While this case wasn't resolved, slaves were later paid for doing similar work.

For twenty guilders of goods plus agreed labors, a slave could also purchase half freedom, allowing blacks to enjoy the full rights of a free person. They were able to marry, have servants, and interact freely with whites. However, this purchased freedom was an illusion. If these blacks failed to make an annual payment or perform the tasks or obligations assigned to them by the West India Company, they were returned to slavery. More importantly, any children born to a half-free couple were considered slaves themselves—ensuring the company a continuing line of profits and labor.

Despite these obstacles, free black communities began to flourish in New Amsterdam. To create a buffer zone between the outpost of New Amsterdam and warring native tribes, the Dutch offered individual blacks land grants on two hundred acres between Canal and Thirty-Fourth Streets. By the late 1640s, thirteen Africans including Simon Congo and Peter Santomee owned farms. Eventually twelve black women became landowners during this period too. Markets that sprang up in this ***bouwerij*** (meaning "farm"), or Bowery, section of the colony were a lively combination of Dutch and African traditions. They were a melting pot where Native American, black, and white settlers interacted socially. These markets were a crossroads of cultures with English, Norwegian, French, German, and Jewish immigrants all participants. Pinkster festivals were a Dutch tradition held each spring. A solemn Dutch holiday turned into a joyous event through African customs. Celebrations included blending the music and dances of Africans and Europeans into a new entertainment that was uniquely American. By Jennings's time, Pinkster fests were widely celebrated by African Americans, and they still are today.

During the fifty-five years of Dutch rule, 306 Africans were taken from their homeland and brought to New Amsterdam while another seventy-five lived there as free people. Roughly 10 percent of the colony's residents were black. Under the lenient Dutch half-free policy, Lucas Santomee, the son of one of the original slaves, grew up to be a well-known and respected doctor. Dorothy d'Angola became the first African in the New World to adopt a child.

Dutch rule and way of life came to an end on a September morning in 1664 when four British warships unexpectedly sailed into New Amsterdam harbor. Dutch governor Peter Stuyvesant took one look at the ships, armed with hundreds of marines ready to attack the collapsing walls of his old fort, and surrendered without firing a shot.[4] England began a 119-year reign over Manhattan that ended with the American Revolution.

New Amsterdam became New York, named in honor of the Duke of York, who sponsored the conquest. The change to British rule had a profound effect on the city's black population. It changed the way slavery devolved and how race relations developed over the next three hundred years. It's generally thought that slaves in the northern parts of America didn't rebel because they were treated somewhat better than their counterparts elsewhere. However, a closer look at relations between slaves and masters shows that the same tensions endured no matter where slavery existed.

Even under the Dutch, bondmen sought their freedom. To counteract this movement, the West India Company passed a law in 1643 making it illegal to harbor runaways. Years later, Manhattan slaves who escaped roamed the wharves along the Slip (South Street) and joined gangs such as the Geneva Club, the Smith Fly Boys, and the Long Bridge Boys. They slipped away to Native American villages and fled their masters during work. When the English tightened slave laws, it only heightened the need for freedom.

The legal grounds for institutionalizing lifetime slavery began in the British Colony of Virginia. Not surprisingly, it coincided with the rise of the tobacco plantations in the 1640s, when labor was scarce and the demand for tobacco was high. The English transitioned from a system of indentured servitude to sanctioning African enslavement.

John Casor was delivered into slavery on the word of his black employer, Anthony Johnson. Johnson was among the Virginia Colony's original twenty settlers. Once indentured himself, he had prospered and owned a five-hundred-acre tobacco farm.[5] Casor claimed he was already indentured to Johnson for fourteen years, twice as long as he agreed to.

Casor proceeded to sell his services to a neighbor. Johnson brought Casor and the neighbor to court, claiming it was understood that Casor's indenture to him was for life.

Based on testimony from a Captain Goldsmith and others, the court "ordered that the said John Casor Negro forthwith returne unto the service of his said master Anthony Johnson."[6] With little fanfare, America was hurtling down the path toward a slavocracy and the four hundred years of racial tensions and civil unrest it wrought. In 1670, when Johnson died, his tobacco farm was granted to a white man instead of his family—he was no longer considered a citizen of the land he once helped settle.

By 1711, the Royal African Company had built a slave market on Wall Street. Slave commerce and the profits it brought to the city's growing merchant class led to laws that made selling people as easy as any product on the market. In the last quarter of the seventeenth century, slaves in New York City had to carry street passes; they couldn't leave their owner's homes or gather in groups of four or more.

The British class system put blacks and slaves on its bottom rung, below white indentured servants. Unlike slaves, indentured people, primarily of Irish, British, Scottish, and German descent, could purchase their freedom. They signed a contract to work for a master for three to seven years. An indentured agreement was seen as a way for the lower classes to afford the trip to America or as payment to learn a skilled labor once there. More than half of the immigrants in the British colonies were indentured to the upper classes, causing economic and social tension between free blacks and their indentured European counterparts. Both groups were competing for the same limited space in British society.

Slaves were banned from learning or practicing any skilled trades. Limitations were placed on the amount, distance, and time slaves traveled. Masters had the right to life or death over their slave property without fear of the law. Towns appointed "Negro whippers" to flog violators. Even in death there was separation. In 1650, the African Burial Ground was established in lower Manhattan, and it was used through the early nineteenth century.

Coupled with the stricter laws aimed at protecting investments in human flesh was an increase in the number of slaves in Manhattan. At the beginning of the eighteenth century, 40 percent of the city's homes owned slaves. As the century progressed, the number of slaves arriving at the Great Dock near the end of Broadway outnumbered incoming Europeans.

This influx of slave labor created a powder keg of resentment and desperation that exploded in violent revolts for freedom. Two of the more horrific uprisings in New York City occurred within twenty-nine years of each other and left an indelible mark on the black and white populations.

On April 6, 1712, twenty-four slaves secretly gathered at midnight and set fire to the home of Peter van Tilburgh near the Maiden Lane orchard. Armed with muskets, swords, and axes, they attacked any white New Yorkers who came to put out the fire. Nine whites were killed and six wounded in the uprising before the local militia stepped in and stopped the violence. Many whites thought the city was close to being ransacked and destroyed by the attack.

Some of the rebels escaped into the forest. Six killed themselves rather than be captured. Altogether seventy black men were dragged off to jail. Of the twenty-seven to face trial, twenty-one were convicted and sentenced to die at Execution Grounds near the African burial plot on the edge of town. Nineteen were put to death by hanging or burning before New York's governor stopped the killings. It was the first organized slave rebellion in North America, and the English dealt with it harshly.

Manumission—the act of freeing a person from slavery—was more expensive after the 1712 revolt. The revised rules called for a master to post a two-hundred-pound bond to free a slave. Freedom was even less likely now. Slaveholding New Yorkers feared that the stricter laws would lead to another insurrection, further heightening the paranoia of whites.

Some historians have compared the panic that gripped New York in 1741 as similar to that of the Salem witch trials fifty years earlier. The city was ripe for hysteria. England was at war with France and Spain, depressing the local economy. There were food shortages and unrest among the lower classes, including slaves, who were now 20 percent of the city's population.

That spring a number of unexplained fires broke out in Fort George (formerly Fort Amsterdam), consuming its chapel, barracks, and the governor's mansion. Another fire began at Captain Warren's home far from the fort, as well as at storehouses and other locations around the city. It seemed that as one fire was put out another started.

Remembering the events of 1712, white New Yorkers were already talking about a slave conspiracy. The testimony of white indentured servant Mary Burton against her master, John Hughson, proved this theory to many. In exchange, she was granted her freedom and a reward. A tavern owner who served blacks and was sympathetic to slaves, Hughson was seen as a likely ringleader for the plot.

In proceedings that were much like the witch trials, Burton began to name every black she knew as a conspirator. For the most part, her word was enough to get a conviction. John Roosevelt—Claes van Rosenvelt's grandson—owned a slave called Quack who was one of the revolt's leaders. Throughout the summer 154 blacks were arrested, along with many whites. Thirteen of them, including Quack, were burned to death; another twenty-two were hanged. In all, thirty-five people were executed, among them Hughson and three other whites.

No one will ever really know if there was a true conspiracy or not. Perceptions of the events of 1741 have changed over the years along with Americans' view of race relations. At one time the white ruling class thought the Africans lacked the intelligence to plan such a wide revolt. Recently we have learned that slaves developed highly sophisticated ways to communicate without speaking the same language. Songs, hand signals, and a dialect of English called pidgin allowed abducted Africans to plan openly in front of their unsuspecting masters.

The events of 1712 and 1741 marked a turning point in the city's race relations. Free blacks were looked down upon as coconspirators and no better than slaves. The stifling new slave codes were aimed at isolating and controlling free and enslaved Africans. Slavery was ill suited for the urban landscape New York was becoming. City life demanded close contact with many peoples and a variety of skilled laborers—both problems for slaveholders. Manhattan's slave population never again reached the peak it saw in the mid-eighteenth century.

By 1807, the United States banned importing slaves.

If owning a slave was no longer profitable or practical in New York City, providing Southern plantation owners with the means to buy their slaves was a growing venture. As the use of slave labor began to wane in Manhattan, the city created a new role for itself as the financial might behind the slave trade.

Many Manhattan businesses turned the gears of slavery by insuring the lives of slaves, trading for cotton and sugar produced by slave labor, or funding the illegal slave ships used to capture a free people.

According to the *Guardian*, about 35 percent of the Nautilus Insurance Company's early business was insuring slaves. This firm later became New York Life. Two banks, now part of JPMorgan Chase, owned 1,250 slaves and took another 13,000 people as payment for plantation loans. Three German brothers opened a Manhattan office, purchased slaves, and swapped slave-picked cotton for cash. Thus, Lehman Brothers was born.

The Havemeyers & Elder sugar refinery built a monopoly on Cuban slave-harvested sugar in the early nineteenth century. Eventually the company moved to Brooklyn and became Domino Sugar—its signage was a waterfront landmark for nearly a hundred years. Sugar and cotton provided such lucrative markets for Manhattan that by the mid-1850s the Ostend Circular called for the United States to annex Cuba as a slave state, a move supported by New York City's mayor and administration.

According to historian Frederic Bancroft, in 1850 the average price for a slave was $400. A decade later, a prime male field hand cost $1,800 depending upon the location. Each child a slave mother gave birth to added about $200 to her value. On average, slave women bore nine offspring. These children, in turn, could be sold for $400 to $500 when they were between the ages of eight and twelve.

To put those numbers into perspective, the average daily wage in 1850 was about $1. Carpenters earned $2.09 a day, or about $300 a year. Free farm hands earned 36 cents for a day's pay, or $140 a year. Skilled laborers could earn up to $600 to $700 annually. In the northeast, milk was 5 cents a quart and oranges 28 cents a dozen. A loaf of bread and a bottle of whiskey sold for 7 cents apiece.

Slavery was a profitable investment, as this 1859 editorial that appeared in the *New-York Daily Tribune* highlights:

> *The man who swindles his fellow creature in the banking, brokering or other business, is very easily reconciled to the slave trade. It will pay magnificently, or at least it does in seven cases out of ten . . . I know of two ladies, who invested in a little venture of this kind not so long ago,*

and as a result have augmented their banking accounts—one to the extent of $23,000 and the other $16,000.

New York City's flourishing illegal slave trade was a major reason for such high investment hopes. Manhattan's deepwater harbor proved to be an asset too. By 1850, lower Manhattan had sixty piers on the East River and fifty more on the Hudson. On any day there might be five hundred ships in New York's harbor. With so many vessels moving in and out of the harbor, it was hard to catch anyone.

Called the "Street of Ships," South Street was the Broadway of the ocean. A walk along its busy network of piers, wharves, and slips was a riotous carnival of chaos. The famous Webb-Eckfor, Bergh-Westervelt,

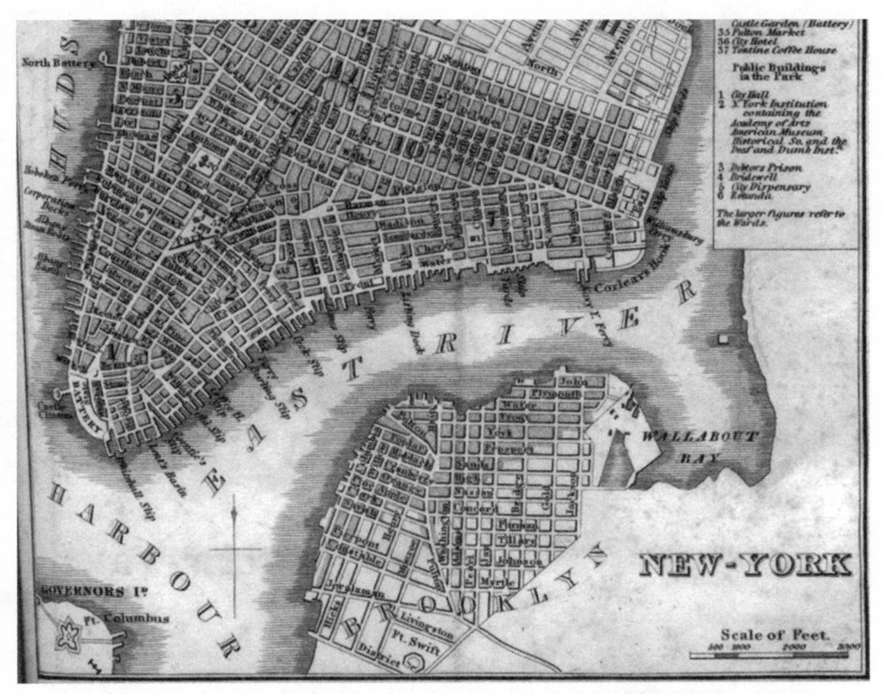

Manhattan's deepwater harbor with its many wharves and piers fueled the illegal slave trade. COURTESY UNIVERSITY OF TEXAS LIBRARIES, THE UNIVERSITY OF TEXAS AT AUSTIN

and Brown-Bell shipyards loomed over the East River. The sound of shipwrights hammering and shaping vessels out of oak rang over the din of ironworkers, food hawkers, and dockworkers. Ship masts rose from the water like mighty forests, in sharp contrast to the low hovels of brick countinghouses on Schermerhorn Row.

Known as the "Street of Ships," South Street served as a base for kidnappers and slavers. THE EDWARD W. C. ARNOLD COLLECTION OF NEW YORK PRINTS, MAPS AND PICTURES, BEQUEST OF EDWARD W. C. ARNOLD, 1954

Estimates show that a single slave voyage could produce a 250 percent profit for its investors. At the 1854 trial of slave ship captain James Smith, he reported that his ship cost $13,000 while his cargo of slaves was worth $220,000. As in many of these cases, Smith burned his vessel afterward to destroy evidence and collect insurance.

In memoirs published in 1864, he states that in 1859 alone eighty-five slavers originated from Manhattan carrying between 30,000 and 60,000 Africans. Smith left no doubt about the city's role in supporting slavery:

New York is the chief port in the world for the Slave Trade. It is the greatest place in the universe for it. Neither in Cuba nor in the Brazils is it carried on so extensively. Ships that convey Slaves to the West Indies and South America are fitted out in New York. Now and then one sails from Boston and Philadelphia; but New York is our headquarters.

Although Smith was found guilty of a capital crime, he received only a two-year sentence and a thousand-dollar fine. New Yorkers chose to look the other way. The "Old Merchant" Moses Taylor, John Jacob Astor, and Junius Morgan—J.P. Morgan's father—all cornerstones of capitalism, made their fortunes from the slave economy, as did many of the city's most successful early residents, the ones who had streets named after them. The Bayard, Stuyvesant, and Van Cortlandt families owned or enslaved humans for personal wealth. Provincial New York governor Gerardus Beekman traded slaves, as did James Duane, Joseph Reade, and Zebulon Pike. Their namesake roadways live on in Google Maps as reminders of a not-so-quaint past when generations of free people were bought and sold for gold.

The human toll from slavery was a heavy one. Most estimates show that 20 percent or more of slaves died during the cruel journey to America, their bodies dumped overboard like garbage. Surviving was equally harsh. When the New York City vessel *Wildfire* was captured off the coast of Florida in 1860, this firsthand account appeared in *Harper's Weekly*:

Young girls, in Nature's dress, some sitting on the floor and others on the lockers, and some sick ones lying in the berths. Four or five of them were a good deal tattooed on the back and arms, and we noticed that three had an arm branded with the figure "7," which, we suppose, is the merchant's mark.

With Northern states taking 40 cents of every dollar earned from Southern cotton, the country seemed content. A give-and-take relationship developed among three key economies—America's, Europe's, and Africa's. Ships outfitted to transport slaves left New York for Europe with sugar, cotton, and tobacco. Manufactured goods picked up in Europe left for the African coast to be traded for enslaved people being hauled against their will to the Americas.

The triangle slave trade—in existence for nearly three hundred years—seemed to work profitably for everyone except the slaves. Increasingly, the country's expansionist yearnings put the economic needs of individual states on a collision course with the idealism expressed in the Declaration of Independence.

The passage of the Fugitive Slave Act as part of the Compromise of 1850 made the United States a slavocracy if it wasn't already. The Act gave the federal government the right to capture runaway slaves in states where slavery was abolished and return them to their owners. In reality, its powers were much more far-reaching. Once captured, alleged fugitives were not allowed to testify or hire a lawyer.

Commissioners had the authority to issue certificates that placed any black person into slavery without evidence. They received ten dollars for issuing these certificates and only five dollars for setting a captive free. If white persons refused to help capture a slave, they could be fined one thousand dollars. This served to galvanize opposition to slavery among white Northerners who were not yet committed to the anti-slavery cause.

Before the Fugitive Slave Act was passed, in 1850, Thomas Jennings, David Ruggles, Charles Ray, and others formed the New York Vigilance Committee to help fugitive slaves establish themselves after escaping. It provided housing, clothing, and money. Increasingly, the committee found itself being called upon to protect the basic human rights of free blacks. With the Fugitive Slave Act, it was war on African Americans; kidnapping was rampant and state-sanctioned. The Ladies Literary Clubs raised money to purchase freedom to help protect people at risk.

On July 5, 1852, before the Ladies' Anti-Slavery Society in Rochester, New York, Frederick Douglass addressed the Fugitive Slave Act by asking, "What to the slave is the Fourth of July?" In discussing the law, he said:

> *Slavery has been nationalized in its more horrible and revolting form . . . By that act, Mason & Dixon's line has been obliterated; New York has become as Virginia; and the power to hold, hunt, and sell men,*

women, and children as slaves remains no longer a mere state institution, but is now an institution of the whole United States.

If Manhattanites thought they could profit from slavery without getting their hands dirty, the Fugitive Slave Act threw a fresh coat of mud on their doorstep. Because the city was a central point on the Underground Railroad for freed slaves heading north on the Hudson River, it was swarming with slave hunters.

They were called skip tracers, but referred to themselves as "blackbirders," and to the African Americans they pursued as "black ivory." South Street was their main corridor. Their favorite place to exchange information was a seafood restaurant on the corner of Fulton and South Streets owned by Freemason Abraham M. Sweet, simply called Sweets. With a hotel upstairs and a saloon next door, Sweets was the perfect location to slip in and out of unnoticed.

The deep-rooted mistrust of law enforcement by the black community has its origins in this period. Here the likes of Manhattan constable Tobias Boudinot and Richard Riker, the recorder of New York City, directed the notorious New York Kidnapping Club. Also included were transplanted Virginians F.H. Pettis, Edward R. Waddy, and John Lyon. The cunning group often had its members pose as abolitionists to lure unsuspecting free blacks and escaping slaves into captivity. Riker and his ancestors owned the island where the city's infamous prison was built in 1932.

Among their most daring attempts was a plot to abduct New York Vigilance Committee secretary David Ruggles. The bold escapade was made to intimidate as much as it was to succeed. A Jennings neighbor and business associate, Ruggles established the New York Vigilance Committee along with Thomas Jennings and others to aid runaway slaves and protect African Americans from abductions. His relentless pursuit of the kidnappers put a fifty-thousand-dollar bounty on his head.

The Kidnappers Club came to Ruggles's home one night in late 1835 and attempted to put him on a steamer bound for Georgia. A slight and often sickly man, Ruggles managed to squirm away at the last minute. He escaped, thwarting "a conspiracy to sacrifice me on the altar of slavery," stated Ruggles in a letter published in the *New York American*. Although Ruggles outsmarted the kidnappers, their audacious act showed free blacks that no one was safe in the city. Even well-known African Americans could be targeted.

The plight of fugitive slaves was high drama and well covered by the white and black press. All the New York papers regularly covered these abductions. The first victim of the Fugitive Slave Act was James Hamilton Williams, also known as James Hamlet. He was arrested in New York just eight days after the law went into effect in September 1850. He was brought before newly appointed commissioner Alexander Gardiner and said he was free because his mother was born free. His testimony was not allowed, and he was taken by the agent of Mary Brown from Baltimore, who claimed him as her slave.

Hamlet was removed from his Williamsburg home without being allowed to speak to his wife or two children. Within five days, fifteen hundred people met at the Zion Chapel and raised five hundred dollars toward his release. White merchants and abolitionists raised another three hundred dollars to meet the sum demanded for his freedom. Hamlet returned to New York and was greeted by a rally of nearly five thousand white and black residents before a parade escorted him home.

Others were not quite as lucky.

Abduction was a very real fear for African Americans in Manhattan and elsewhere in the country. As early as 1839, educator and activist Theodore D. Weld commented, "It is a notorious fact that large numbers of free colored persons are kidnapped every year in the Free States, taken to the South, and sold as slaves."

Schoolchildren were in the most danger of kidnapping. Well-off black families like that of Elizabeth Jennings often educated their children in private schools that had constant supervision to prevent problems. Black clergy from Manhattan and Brooklyn banded together in 1851 to determine how to face the growing kidnapping issue. Surprisingly, they recommended that young black men form "military companies" to protect themselves and their families. Their cries for help to the police went unanswered.

The world Elizabeth Jennings inherited from America's forefathers was a dark and treacherous one. There was no shining light on the hill to cut through the gloom of racism and greed that enveloped her city. As she rushed down Church Street, the organist was determined to lead her choir. The voices of her community would be heard, but perhaps not in the way she imagined.

Chapter IV

Bold Men of Color

Our claims are on America. It is the land that gave us birth; it is the land of our nativity, we know no other country.

—Thomas L. Jennings,
Oration

Saturday night, July 12, 1834, was nearly moonless. The moon was in a waxing phase; the old-timers would say it foretold of a shift coming, a call to action. The approaching dusk turned the flat-roofed clapboard and brick buildings of lower Manhattan into tombstone shadows. The absence of light brought with it a shadowy tide that oozed and congealed from the wharves of the old city. It crept uptown like a river rat along the damp stone walls and twisted back alleys, flowing into a single riotous white mob thousands strong.

Only a lone watchman's lamp flickering across the caramel skin of young Elizabeth Jennings reflected any light inside her family home at 35 Chatham Street. The darkened avenue of commerce made it hard for the rioters to distinguish one address from another. That night white residents were told to light a candle in a window and stand behind it to ensure their homes wouldn't be touched by violence. Jennings and other black businessmen had to ask the city for an "application for protection of the premises" to try to keep their families safe.

What became known as the Abolitionist Riots began two days earlier, on Wednesday, July 9, 1834, when an angry mob gathered at the Chatham Street Chapel. (Other sources refer to these riots as the Farren, Tappan, or July Riots as well.) These riots erupted suddenly yet were building for years. It all began one Sunday in mid-June 1834 when white parishioners of the Brick Presbyterian Church were outraged after abolitionist Arthur Tappan invited black minister and newspaper publisher Samuel Cornish to sit in his pew. To calm his churchgoers, the pastor, Dr. Samuel Cox, called for unity and pointed out that Jesus himself may have been darker-skinned than the congregation that sat before him. His statement was too much for the editor of the *New York Commercial Advertiser*. He wrote an article that helped spur the public to violent action.

> *The result is Dr. Cox alleges our Saviour was a negro—an averment as revolting to the moral sense of the community as it is distant from historic truth . . . For if Dr. Cox, and other kindred visionaries, whose intellectual aberrations entitle them to the sympathy & protection of their friends . . . the pulpit will cease either to deserve or receive deference and respect.*

On the other end of the spectrum were the Tappan brothers, Arthur and Lewis. Born two years apart in Northampton, Massachusetts, they came to Manhattan to make their way in the world after working in their father's dry goods store. They quickly made a vast fortune as silk importers. Then they established the *New York Journal of Commerce*, along with Samuel Morse, which still exists today (it was an odd pairing considering Morse's racist views and the Tappans' abolitionism). The credit rating agency they started in 1841 eventually became Dun and Bradstreet. Arthur Tappan owned a massive granite three-story dry goods store at 122 Pearl Street near Hanover Square.

Although successful at commerce, the Tappans believed their main role in life was to save souls. They saw the wicked sin of slavery hanging over America as the biggest impediment to salvation. The Tappans, along with Gerrit Smith and other white donors, put their considerable financial resources behind the abolitionist movement. By sponsoring numerous local chapters of the American Anti-Slavery Society and funding abolitionist publications for children and adults, the Tappans became the face of American abolitionism. In 1839, Lewis took on a major role in freeing the slaves brought to trial during the *Amistad* case before the Supreme Court.

However, it should be underscored that all across America, black philanthropists such as Stephen Smith, Henry C. Thompson, and Bridget "Biddy" Mason did the heavy everyday lifting of freeing, educating, employing, and providing community support for the formerly enslaved. Their grassroots actions showed in the mastery of how the Underground Railroad was connected; it was built by local folks who knew how to get around unnoticed. In the Empire City that role was filled by Thomas L. Jennings and his associates. Among them were the Reverends J.W.C. Pennington, Samuel Cornish, Peter Williams Jr., and David Ruggles.

Today we would call them a cross-functional team of entrepreneurs, religious leaders, and agents for social change. Back then they were what Frederick Douglass referred to as "bold men of color." Their boldness was an affront to the white power structure of the city that also made them marked men during the Abolitionist Riots.

View of Broadway in 1834 with Trinity Church in the background. COURTESY NEW YORK PUBLIC LIBRARY

The Chatham Street Chapel wasn't always a place of worship. It opened in 1824 toward the back of a public green near City Hall as the Chatham Gardens Theater. With a large, open, floor-level stage, it somewhat resembled the minor league sports arenas of today. In 1833, the Tappans purchased the building and turned it into an evangelical church where all races, sexes, and faiths could worship in harmony. Abolitionist speakers such as Charles Grandison Finney, John Pendleton Kennedy, and Theodore Weld lectured there and attended American Anti-Slavery Society meetings.

On the Fourth of July in 1834, a choir of black and white singers celebrated the holiday with an anti-slavery hymn written by John Greenleaf Whittier. He wrote the hymn for them, only to have it disrupted by pro-slavery insurgents in the audience. Their thuggery broke up the service. It was rescheduled at the chapel for Monday, July 7.

As the pro-slavery *New York Daily Advertiser* explained, the all-white New York Sacred Music Society rented the chapel on Monday and Thursday nights to practice. When the music society showed up, the anti-slavery event was already underway. According to a reporter from the *New York Daily Advertiser*:

> *When they came, they found it already preoccupied by a large congregation of blacks of both sexes . . . in order to hear a sermon from a colored man named Hughes. [They were asked to leave,] but without avail, as the blacks obstinately refused to remove . . . aroused, and they struck Dr. Rockwell, Mr. Clark and others with canes loaded with leaden bullets on the head, knocked down some and injured others severely.*

Outraged by the attacks, the newspaper reported, the whites had to defend themselves. Watchmen were called and closed down the chapel. The *New York Observer* was even blunter, describing abolitionists as a group "that endangers the safety of the south and the union of the States. This is true . . . abolitionists are wild and reckless incendiaries."

Not all the city's newspapers saw it that way. The *Evening Post* called out several inflammatory papers in what would be called an editorial today.

> *The violent tirades of certain prints opposed to the Abolitionists—the Commercial Advertiser and Courier and Enquirer in particular. With regard to the last print, the direct tendency and we fear the purpose also, of several of its articles was to kindle public feeling against certain individuals who take a prominent part in the Abolition cause.*

On the evening of July 9 the cauldron boiled over. Worked into a frenzy by false accounts that abolitionists favored mixed marriage, and already agitated by African American Jubilation Day celebrations marking the seventh anniversary of slavery ending in New York, white pro-slavery citizens took to the streets. Three mobs gathered that night, the first at the Chatham Street Chapel. They trashed the building, attacking any black person they saw. Emboldened, the rabble turned farther downtown to deal with the building's owner. Lewis Tappan's unoccupied brick home was at 40 Rose Street.

They looted, smashed windows, tossed his furniture into a barn fire, and destroyed his property. The frenzy only abated when someone was about to heave a portrait of George Washington onto the fire, and according to accounts from the day, the rioters began shouting, "For God's sake, don't burn Washington!" The portrait was rescued. Afterward, Tappan's wife put on a brave face by saying they wanted to get rid of a lot of the furniture anyway. Tappan never moved back and left the charred remains of his home as a reminder of crowd madness.

Several blocks away, another theater was attacked on Bowery Road. George Farren, a British stage manager, allegedly fired an American actor and made comments sympathetic to abolitionists. Farren quickly apologized and sated the crowd by having the performers sing popular racist and patriotic songs.

The next day, the *Commercial Advertiser* took another dig at the abolitionists; this whole situation was laid at their doorstep. "Abolitionists are the worst enemies the blacks of this city have. They are holding out to them the prospect of amalgamation, feeding their pride with impractical hopes."

At the same time, the *Commercial Advertiser* tried to walk back its previous comments, claiming,

> *We profess to live under a government of laws, and the sanctity of private habitation and repose shall not be violated . . . Let every lover of the city's peace put his face against every movement calculated to disturb it.*

It was not to be. From July 9 to 12, 1834, thousands of pro-slavery Manhattanites attacked the churches, looted the businesses, and destroyed the homes of noted abolitionists. Early on there was some sense of comeuppance toward the abolitionists. The riots continued on Thursday night, July 10, with another vandalistic raid on Tappan's deserted home, an attack on Reverend Cox's residence at 3 Charlton Street, as well as one on his Brick Presbyterian Church, primarily attended by white parishioners. Suddenly things seemed to be getting out of hand. New Yorkers watching safely from the sidelines felt threatened by mob violence.

Finally, on Friday, July 11, Mayor Cornelius Lawrence issued a proclamation that despite the repulsion of the abolitionists it was in everyone's best interest not to assemble in crowds. No one listened. As darkness fell over the city that night, a vicious ugliness was unleashed that couldn't be controlled. There were at least seven major confrontations. Arthur Tappan's store was under siege. He had thirty-six armed employees ready to defend it. What started as a protest had turned into a war, with the government nowhere to be found.

The Spring Street Church was sacked on the rumor that an interracial marriage ceremony took place there. Its pastor's home on Thompson Street was heavily vandalized. The African Society for Mutual Relief hall where the Jubilation Day marches began and Thomas Jennings delivered many of his speeches was destroyed. The St. Philip's and the African Baptist Churches, along with dozens of black-owned business and homes, were also part of the wreckage. The quaint streets now resembled a war zone the likes of which the city had not seen since the American Revolution.

At the intersection of Spring and Varick Streets, the mob overturned wagons and piled tables and wooden debris high to create barricades. Gleeful in their defiance, the throng cheered themselves, only to have Major General Jacob Morton order his cavalry to charge the bastions and disperse the crowd.

On Saturday, July 12, a list of potential riot targets was compiled by the mayor's office with the aid of informants. Mayor Lawrence issued another proclamation, as found in the *New York Journal of Commerce*, "[I] hereby require and command all good citizens to unite in aid of the civil authorities, to put an end to these disreputable occurrences."

It was no longer just disenfranchised blacks without voting rights who were targets. The gleaming new Colonnade Row Greek Revival town houses at Lafayette Place were pegged for destruction because they were built using stone cut by prison labor rather than paid stonecutters. The State Arsenal on Elm Street and Bridewell's Prison behind City Hall were selected to be torched as symbols of government power. The list of targeted locations swelled to more than thirty-five. Among them were the residences of African American activists Thomas Jennings, Rev. Peter Williams Jr., and the "Oyster King," Thomas Downing, on Broad Street.

Once again, the 27th Regiment was called out to quell the violence, only this time the militia had orders to shoot any rioters who turned around to fight. The cavalry patrolled the streets on horseback to further deter the horde. It must have been difficult for Jennings the inventor and tailor to watch his neighborhood be destroyed by the very people who sought his services on a daily basis. Ready to defend the city during the War of 1812, Jennings now saw the New Yorkers he had worked with hand in hand to save the city from the British twenty-two years before looting it themselves.

That night, any sounds of breaking glass, war whoops, or screams would have brought the Jennings family to its feet. Instead, in the distance, they heard the rhythmic thumping of marching. As reported by historian Joel T. Headley, "The sheen of nearly a thousand bayonets made the street look like a lane of steel." Heavy rain later that night finally put a damper on the raging fires and the hateful rhetoric.

As the sun rose the next morning, people left the safety of their cellars and attics to survey the damage to their homes and businesses. The extent of the riot's devastation was evident at every street corner as neighbors consoled one another. Although spared, Elizabeth's family felt the aftereffects of the destruction. Rioters ransacked St. Philip's again, where Elizabeth's siblings once attended school in the church's undercroft. They burned the parish's furniture in the street and smashed its beautiful thousand-dollar organ to bits. In all, seven churches were destroyed along with dozens of homes, and there were untold personal injuries.

Though thousands rioted, only several dozen arrests were reported in newspapers. At least nine rioters were sentenced to hard labor on Blackwell's Island; others went scot-free or received lenient sentences. The closest thing to an apology to black citizens came from the *Journal of Commerce*, which stated: "They have given no provocation and have borne their injuries with commendable patience."

Those African Americans who were free faced overwhelming hardships and prejudices just trying to obtain equal citizenship, if that was even possible. The thought of emigrating to another land that promised equality was debated and explored by black leaders.

Called the African colonization movement, the idea had strong support among white elite political leaders. Slaveholders Thomas Jefferson, James Monroe, and Henry Clay were all proponents of creating a separate country for free blacks. Francis Scott Key, who also owned slaves, was on the American Colonization Society board. Twelve of the first eighteen presidents owned slaves.

Abraham Lincoln supported the colonization movement with Clay. At Clay's memorial service on July 6, 1852, Lincoln's eulogy put forth the colonization concept as a way to honor the late Kentuckian.

> *If as the friends of colonization hope, the present and coming generations of our countrymen shall by any means, succeed in freeing our land from the dangerous presence of slavery; and, at the same time, in restoring a captive people to their long-lost father-land, with bright prospects for the future; and this too, so gradually, that neither races nor individuals shall have suffered by the change, it will indeed be a glorious consummation. And if, to such a consummation, the efforts of Mr. Clay shall have contributed, it will be what he most ardently wished, and none of his labors will have been more valuable to his country and his kind.*

Many early abolitionists such as Arthur Tappan and Gerrit Smith also were originally colonizationists. Racism was a major factor in the group's existence.

In the beginning, there was widespread support for the American Colonization Society among important black leaders such as the Rev. Peter Williams of New York, Rev. Daniel Coker of Baltimore, and James Forten, Bishop Richard Allen, and Rev. Absalom Jones, all of Philadelphia. It made sense on a certain level because the ACS plan was similar to a mission that wealthy black shipowner Paul Cuffee undertook in Sierra Leone, and he was looking for support.

In January 1817, a convention of three thousand black delegates from around the country was held at the Bethel A.M.E Church in Philadelphia. It was James Forten's home turf, and the leaders were looking to seal the deal with the group's support. Thomas Jennings and many of the New York abolitionists were among them. But instead of conformation, they got confrontation. In a letter to Cuffee, Forten wrote, "Not one sole [*sic*] was in favor of going to Africa." To a man, no one was for colonization. After a second meeting that summer with the same result, the leadership joined their brothers and stood unified in their opposition to the colonization movement.

Colonization was the shiny object for Americans who wanted to reap the economic benefits of slavery but not have to confront its grisly reality every day. Like the hidden doors and hallways of Jefferson's home, Monticello, colonization could make slavery guiltless, efficient, and invisible. No one understood this better than William Lloyd Garrison, who knew that the biggest threat to slavery was a successful and vibrant black working class.

In 1832, he wrote *Thoughts on African Colonization*. Indirectly, the book led to William Arthur's conversion to abolitionism and likely influenced his son's interest in defending anti-slavery and civil rights clients. Garrison's friendship and alliance with the Manhattan abolitionists was cemented when Jennings, Peter Williams Jr., Thomas Sipkins, and William Hamilton donated funds to get the book published. Garrison had this to say about why slaveholders wanted free blacks "expatriated."

> *'Free blacks contaminate your slaves, excite their deadliest hate, and are a source of horrid danger to yourselves! They must be removed, or your destruction is inevitable.' What is their response? Precisely such as might be expected—We know it; we dread the presence of this class; their influence over our slaves weakens our power, and endangers our safety; they must, they shall be expatriated, or be crushed to the earth if they remain!*

To get his anti-colonization treatise published, William Lloyd Garrison turned to New York's "bold men of color" for financing.
SOUTHWORTH AND HAWES (AMERICAN, ACTIVE 1843–1863)

Thomas Jennings and Manhattan's bold men of color were among the earliest and most effective of the black anti-colonization speakers. They expressed the complicated relationship between African Americans, their county, and their ancestry in a way that white empathizers such as Garrison and Tappan couldn't. From the Colonization Society's start, black New Yorkers questioned its motives and logic. They saw an unstable Liberian government that was controlled by the white colonizationists, battles with native Africans over land, and a high death rate for the black settlers as reasons not to support the movement. These leaders also suspected that the Colonization Society planned for the forcible deportation of all free blacks.

In New York City, two enclaves emerged that demonstrated that African American–run towns could thrive on their own, or as part of an integrated community. When the Lefferts family purchased nearly all of central Brooklyn, it was hard to imagine the heavily forested area the British could barely navigate during the Revolution would one day be farmland.

Decades later, when John Lefferts was selling property on the eastern part of the family land, black real estate developer Henry C. Thompson saw it as an opportunity to help African Americans become property owners. He bought thirty-two lots. The first two were purchased by stevedore James Weeks. The community that grew around him would bear his name, Weeksville. By the 1850s, more than five hundred African Americans called Weeksville home. It had its own churches, businesses, and schools.

Across the river in upper Manhattan, a similar village emerged during the mid-1820s when John and Elizabeth Whitehead began selling off their farm in lots. This land was beyond the outskirts of the city, between Eighty-Second and Eighty-Seventh Streets where Seventh and Eighth Avenues are today. It was just west of where the Croton Reservoir would be built twelve years later. The first person to make a purchase, on September 25, 1825, was a young African American boot polisher, Andrew Williams. He took three lots for $125. Next came Epiphany Davis. She threw down her money for twelve lots, while the African Methodist Episcopal Zion Church took six lots to use as a cemetery. Over the next decade, the Whiteheads sold about forty lots to African Americans.

It was the beginning of Seneca Village, one of the first communities settled by black landowners. For black males to vote, they needed to hold the title to $250 worth of land. By 1850, 10 percent of the city's voting black population lived in Seneca Village. The numbers are small; only about one hundred black men were eligible to vote in the city that year. If the settlement kept growing, one day they would be a political force to be reckoned with. The village quickly grew to be home to more than three hundred residents. It had three churches, two schools, and five cemeteries. During the 1830s and 1840s, the population of the village began to diversify as immigrants from Ireland and Germany came to America. Eventually a third of the village's residents were of white European descent. They attended churches together with blacks, shared services such as midwives, and interacted socially with few problems.

Around the same time, other towns across the country were started by African Americans: Brooklyn, Illinois; Fort Mose, Florida; and New Philadelphia, Illinois, to name a few. After the Civil War, more of these sprang up and were called "black towns." The colonizationists were wrong and didn't look very hard to test their theories. Left to their own devices, folks integrated and learned to live together.

Thomas Jennings was among the most outspoken opponents of colonization, as were Peter Williams Jr., the first rector of St. Philip's Church; Samuel Cornish, *Freedom's Journal*'s coeditor; J.W.C. Pennington; and David Ruggles. They each took the colonizationists head-on and made it clear that they weren't going anywhere.

In 1828, Jennings addressed the New York African Society for Mutual Relief, touching upon the core themes that guided his principles about public service and activism, principles that his youngest daughter, Elizabeth, and four other children would live up to throughout their lifetimes. He opened his talk with praise for the working classes of mechanics, farmers, and financiers, declaring that they could all learn something from one another.

However, he quickly challenged the audience, stating "that many of our young men, after acquiring knowledge of letters and numbers . . . bury their talents in the earth and are lost to society." By doing more for the greater community, he added, one can "stand as a bright star in the firmament for generations yet unborn."

He went on to say that if he thought "we would always remain in our degraded state" he would have lived the self-indulgent life of a rich man. Instead, one generation must lead the next. Hard work and education built pride; just "as the constant dropping of water will make an impression on the hardest stone, so will our feeble efforts in time."

After asking his listeners to use self-improvement and community involvement as ways to create a better future, Jennings recalled the proud past of Africa. They were descended from a land of great empires. Hannibal the ancient Carthaginian general and his African soldiers terrorized Europe's Rome. That greatness, he felt, was still within each of them, but their destiny lay elsewhere. His words were reprinted in *Freedom's Journal*:

> *Our claims are on America. It is the land that gave us birth; it is the land of our nativity, we know no other country, it is a land in which our fathers have suffered and toiled; they have watered it with their tears and fanned it with sighs.*

"Africa is as foreign to us as Europe is to them [white Americans]," he added. In the United States, a new Africa could grow "strong and flourish as the Cedars of Lebanon."

Jennings chose his words wisely. Since biblical times, the cedars of Lebanon were known as a particularly good stock of wood. A deep reddish brown, these trees towered over their North American counterparts, spreading their branches far and wide. Jennings saw to it that the roots of those trees had the right soil to grow. He instilled the same values in his family, leading by example. It was one more way for him to demonstrate community pride and responsibility.

After the 1834 Abolitionist Riots ended, Bishop Benjamin Treadwell Onderdonk, who led the Episcopal Diocese of New York, demanded in a very public way that Jennings's good friend Rev. Peter Williams Jr. stop his abolitionist activities. His letter to Williams requiring a public response was sent to several newspapers. Onderdonk was a sourpussed old man who was looking to curtail the involvement of African Americans in Episcopal affairs. He feared controversy at a time when he was hoping to draw richer white congregants into the fold. He should have kept an eye on himself. He was a serial groper accused of making unwanted physical advances on numerous young women and was suspended from his duties in 1845. His brother, also a bishop, was suspended in Pennsylvania for the same issues. Williams capitulated to his superior's demands in a long letter to the public stating that he was trying to do the right thing. He died suddenly six years later, in 1840.

But others were ready to take his place. Samuel Cornish used his editorial skills and positions at the *Freedom's Journal* and *Colored American* newspapers to ensure that the speeches of Jennings, Williams, Hamilton, and others found an audience beyond those who were in the room to hear them. Cornish advocated for better education for blacks and served as a community liaison with the New York African Free School system. In

1840, he coauthored a pamphlet with Theodore Wright called *The Colonization Scheme Considered, in Its Rejection by the Coloured People.*

Earlier, another black Manhattan abolitionist also found success writing pamphlets. David Ruggles, one of the cofounders of the Phoenix Society with Thomas Jennings, didn't have to do much to agitate pro-slavery advocates. He knew how to push their buttons. Born in Norwich, Connecticut, Ruggles worked as a sailor on local waterways before moving to Manhattan in 1827 to open a grocery store on Cortlandt Street. He fit right in with the local black merchants, and soon he was working full-time as an agent for Tappan's *Emancipator* newspaper while writing articles and giving anti-slavery speeches. He started the *Mirror of Liberty*, America's first black magazine, for which William Jennings was an agent in Boston. With his mariner's background, Ruggles confronted sea captains smuggling slaves and fought kidnappers as well.

Among his more successful works was an anti-colonization satire, *The "Extinguisher" Extinguished! Or David M. Reese, M.D., "Used Up," by David Ruggles, a Man of Color.* In it, he took on Dr. David Reese, an administrator for Bellevue Hospital and the city school system, who claimed to oppose slavery but was pro-colonization. Reese mocked the current group of abolitionists as neophytes and published his attack on the American Anti-Slavery Society.

Ruggles responded with a forty-six-page booklet that went right at Reese. He saw himself as Reese's intellectual, moral, and racial equal. Ruggles asked a very modern and poignant question that only a person who has lived with oppression could ask.

> *All History declares that colonization is adverse to the spiritual interests of any country. What are the effects of Christian colonies upon the red men of the forest, the aborigines of America?*

White leaders had no compunction against taking land from indigenous people. They looked down upon those, such as Ruggles, who thought it wrong as inferior. James William Charles Pennington saw the same cognitive dissonance when he became the first African American student to attend Yale College. He couldn't officially enroll, speak, or borrow books, but he could listen "so long as my voice could not be heard."

Being heard would never be an issue for Pennington again. Born a Maryland slave, he escaped and worked as a blacksmith in Newtown, Long Island, before studying theology. Pennington moved to New York City, where he became a pastor and was mentored by Rev. Samuel Cox, whom the newspapers blamed for starting the Abolitionist Riots with his sermons. In the 1840s, Pennington published a well-received autobiography, *The Fugitive Blacksmith,* in England. While in Europe, he purchased his freedom with aid from the Scottish people and earned a doctorate from Heidelberg University in Germany.

He took the position that there was no acceptable form of slavery. Benevolence couldn't be a placebo for freedom and dignity. More than anything, freedom meant self-determination, the right to choose where to live. In 1830, Pennington began attending National Negro Conventions, where he spoke vehemently against colonization, saying, "I am American to the backbone."

His powerful sermons led him to become a convention delegate, with his name appearing alongside those of all the other New Yorkers in meeting minutes. It was a formidable lineup of black middle-class businessmen, religious leaders, and scholars: Williams Jr., Ruggles, Sipkins, Jennings, Pennington, and Cornish. Together on so many committees for so many causes over the years, these men must have enjoyed one another's company.

In September 1838, they faced another challenge. An African American sailor named Stewart knocked on Ruggles's door accompanied by a friend in need. Ruggles and the Vigilance Committee helped some six hundred slaves escape. There was no reason to believe this one would be any different. The young man wanted to wait for his fiancée from Baltimore, so they could immigrate to Canada together. Ruggles invited him to stay for the week and convinced him instead to continue on to the shipyards of New Bedford, Massachusetts, where abolitionism was fervent.

On September 15, 1838, the couple was secretly married in Ruggles's home by the Reverend J.W.C. Pennington. Because of constant surveillance, it's not likely that any of the other "bold men" attended the ceremony. The couple left Manhattan as Mr. and Mrs. Bailey. They would soon be known to the world as Frederick and Anna Douglass.

New York's black abolitionists still faced the daunting if not insurmountable task of trying to simultaneously end slavery, create a civil rights movement, and thwart the colonizationists.

Chapter V

Sisters in Struggle

Arise, put on your armor, ye daughters of America, and start forth in the full field of improvement.

—Mrs. Elizabeth Jennings,
"On the Improvement of the Mind"

THREE DAYS AFTER THE JENNINGS FAMILY CELEBRATED CHRISTMAS IN 1842, AN extraordinary event took place at Armory Hall in Boston, Massachusetts. That Saturday afternoon word quickly spread that a *Christkindleinbaum* was in the great room where an anti-slavery fair was taking place.

Men, women, and children who never gave slavery a thought rushed to the scene. They weren't disappointed at the sight, covered with strings of nuts, glittering apples, pincushions, sugar crystals, and brightly colored paper birds. Bostonians were in awe of their first Christmas tree. So many people jammed into the hall demanding to buy raffle tickets for a chance to win one of its ornaments, the organizers delayed the drawing for several days.

Describing the fair in the January 20, 1843, edition of the *Liberator*, the paper left no doubt who deserved credit for its success: "in every aspect, [the affair was] worthy of the ladies who had so actively prepared for this." What started as a minor living room sale to aid the anti-slavery cause within a few years grew into a colossal fund-raiser bringing in $5,000 annually, the equivalent of roughly $152,000 today.

Similar scenes unfolded in small towns and big cities across the country. In less than a generation, women emerged as a force of change and had a profound influence on the anti-slavery movement. The first women to form abolitionist groups in the 1820s were the wives of the white merchant class. These early reformers saw themselves as extensions of their husband's or father's image. By supporting his charitable work, they were helping expand the power and influence of the family name.

Social restrictions also limited the way women could organize. For example, it was considered improper for women to voice their opinions directly about slavery. Letters to newspapers written by women were signed using only first names so as to not identify the writer. To avoid looking aggressive, women chose passive methods such as raising money that was then donated to male-run organizations.

Race and gender constrained membership as well. Men and women could not belong to the same society or attend meetings together unless specially invited. Ending slavery was viewed as an issue that would be decided by white male abolitionists. This began to change in the 1830s as a new generation of young women banded together. Lucretia Mott and Abby Kelley were among the first women recognized by the male anti-slavery establishment.

In 1833, they along with several other white female activists and black males were invited to attend the first American Anti-Slavery Society meeting in Philadelphia. Asked only to participate as silent "witnesses," these women quickly made their presence known. Within six years, they were asked to join as full members, setting off a backlash from conservative males who believed women were inferior. They didn't think females deserved to be treated as equals. Many white men felt that women, free blacks, and slaves weren't capable of making complex decisions or holding the same jobs they did.

These feelings came to a head at an anti-slavery gathering in Connecticut in 1840. Stopped from speaking by a minister, Kelley challenged him to allow females to be heard. Enraged, the parson shouted, "I will not consent to have women lord it over men in public assemblies. It is enough for women to rule at home." Sexism wasn't confined by race. "Wait till your husband confides in you, and do not give your advice till he asks it," a male-run African American publication suggested. "Always appear flattered by the little he does for you."

Women were able to explore issues, discuss their findings as a group, and develop opinions on their own. To understand slavery and racism better, they turned to a scarcely heard voice. Listening to the physical and verbal abuses black women suffered, white female abolitionists realized they had much in common. Stories of slave mothers trying to protect their children and keep families together drew great sympathy. Their white counterparts saw the fight against bigotry as similar to the sexism they faced every day.

Sarah and Angelina Grimké, renowned abolitionist daughters of a South Carolina slaveholder, read letters from their compatriots of the discrimination they faced. Letters to them from Sarah Mapps Douglass of Philadelphia tell of the humiliation caused while attending a Quaker church service and being forced to sit in a blacks-only pew. In another report, a Massachusetts household had its black servant eat off dishes kept separate from the rest of family's. Sarah Grimké understood discrimination all too well. Her father limited what books she read and forbade her from becoming a lawyer as her brother did because she was female.

Determined to break racism as well as end slavery, women's groups began inviting their black sisters to join them. Increasingly, the movement was about not just freedom but acceptance and tolerance. As Angelina Grimké proclaimed in 1837 at the first Anti-Slavery Convention of American Women in New York City, "the more we mingle with our oppressed brethren and sisters, the more deeply are we convinced of the sinfulness of that anti-Christian prejudice which is crushing them to the earth."

African American women found their voice by putting community first in a way that served people in need, lifted black status, and broadened their influence as reformers. Representing the most successful African American families of the day, these women already felt a tremendous sense of responsibility to their communities. As the wives and daughters of black leaders, they were expected to mirror the ideals of white womanhood while working to defeat slavery and raise a family.

Lacking resources and equal access to education, literary societies blossomed in African American neighborhoods during the 1830s and 1840s. Black women were drawn to these literary societies because they offered them entrance to the world of education and a place to discuss ideas of the day. It was a world of new opportunities they were more than ready to grasp.

During the first public speech ever by an American woman, black activist Maria Stewart put it bluntly. Showing her frustration in Boston's Franklin Hall on September 21, 1832, she questioned the cultural limits placed on black women: "How long, shall the fair daughters of Africa be compelled to bury their minds and their talents beneath a load of iron pots and kettles?"

A typical black female literary society had twenty to thirty members. Annual dues were one or two dollars and used to purchase books. These were lent to members, much like today's libraries. Some large organizations owned as many as six hundred books. To begin meetings, passages from the Bible were read aloud and discussed based on how they related to slavery. Only simple refreshments were served to remind attendees to reflect upon the enslaved.

A portion of each meeting was dedicated to improving writing skills. Essays focused on exposing the injustices that African Americans faced daily. Members submitted articles, poems, and papers anonymously to a committee that read the pieces aloud to the rest of the club. The group then debated the merits of the writing without concern of offending the author. Providing the writer with feedback helped develop analytical thinking among other associates and let the reader practice her public speaking. These skills were necessary to coax an emotional response from audiences and get them to donate money at fund-raisers.

In 1834, Henrietta Ray, Abigail Mathews, Sarah Elston, and Elizabeth's mother were among the founders of the Ladies Literary Society of New York City. Shunned in Boston by both black and white male abolitionists as a radical, Maria Stewart moved to Manhattan and joined the group while teaching school.

Stewart was both pragmatic and evocative when it came to education. She wasn't afraid to poke her audience in the ribs to make a point, as she did in her 1831 pamphlet, ***Religion and the Pure Principles of Morality: The Sure Foundation on Which We Must Build***, when she asked, "What examples have ye set before the rising generation" and "What foundation have ye laid for generations yet unborn?" Stewart saw teachers and mothers as the primary tool to help elevate black stature. It was no accident that many of the daughters of Literary Society members grew up to be outstanding teachers in their own right. Stewart may not have had children of her own, but she helped raise a generation.

Every step toward self-improvement and education put them a step closer to ending slavery. The Literary Society was particularly interested in recruiting and reaching out to young African American women. As a mother, Mrs. Jennings saw the impact racial prejudice had on her children, particularly her three daughters.

Many of the other members had daughters of their own who were with them at these meetings or playing together outside. If their mothers weren't paying attention, the girls might sneak away and begin rhythmically clapping as they formed a large circle for a ring dance. Two of the girls would enter the circle twirling the ends of a rope as two more skipped and danced as they all sang:

> My old mistress promised me,
> Before she dies she would set me free.
> Now she's dead and gone to hell
> I hope the devil will burn her well.

Establishing a literary society was an ambitious and risky undertaking. Calling for black women to educate themselves left the association's members open as targets for ridicule and abuse from whites. Riots, physical cruelty, and kidnapping were common responses to their meetings. Surprisingly, the fledgling African American group received little support from its white counterpart, the Ladies' New York Anti-Slavery Society.

Many white female Manhattanites were content to stand behind their husbands. "We are opposed to the public voting and speaking of women in meetings, to their acting on committees or as officers of the society of men," stated a resolution passed during the group's fifth annual meeting.

They also didn't allow African American women to attend their gatherings. The white anti-slavery group planned to bar black women from the first Anti-Slavery Convention of American Women that they were hosting in New York City. The Grimké sisters, Abby Kelley, and others condemned the prejudice with fiery speeches. Faced with unrelenting pressure, the white anti-slavery group capitulated. In May 1837, a delegation of six black women from the Ladies Literary Society attended the four-day convention along with other black women from around the country.

If it wasn't enough to have white female groups rally against them, African American males also wanted to limit the participation of black and white females in the political process. Formed in 1833, the American Anti-Slavery Society pooled the resources of hundreds of local and state abolitionist groups into a national network.

Despite calls for equality, women weren't allowed to openly join the American Anti-Slavery Society. A select few were permitted to sit as silent partners but were unable to participate, speak on their own, or vote on Society issues.

In 1839, liberal factions of the Society put forth a vote to allow women full participation. Within weeks, the established old guard shot back with a signed declaration protesting "that women have the right of originating, debating and voting on questions which come before the Society."

Among others, Lewis Tappan, Thomas Downing, John Jay, and Thomas L. Jennings signed the document. They would prove to be on the wrong side of history. William Lloyd Garrison and his supporters wanted full membership for women and nominated Abby Kelley to a committee at the 1840 convention, causing such an uproar that the protest signers walked out of the meeting. They formed the female-free American and Foreign Anti-Slavery Society. Kelley and other female activists continued to push for their freedoms and in 1848 held the first Women's Rights Convention in Seneca Falls, New York.

Despite the lack of support and untimely death of the Ladies Literary Society's president, Mrs. Ray, Mrs. Jennings and the society members moved forward with an aggressive agenda. The group continued raising money for the New York Vigilance Committee and other community causes.

They petitioned the US Congress to abolish slavery in the nation's capital. Petitioning Congress was perhaps the most visible and important contribution of the women's anti-slavery movement. During the mid-1830s, millions of petitioned names calling for an end to slavery flooded Congress. The purpose was to stir debate and remind elected officials about the evils of slavery. The female New Yorkers were among the first to circulate petitions. It was dangerous work that required going door-to-door in a hostile and riotous city. Even after getting thousands of signatures in support of the petition, in 1836, Congress reacted by passing a "gag rule" on debating petitions to end slavery.

To complement their successful petition campaign, the Ladies Literary Society used the "free labor" movement to raise cash. They only sold items made from raw materials that weren't produced by slave labor. Free labor showed that the American economy didn't need slavery to exist. It also pointed out to everyday people how they unknowingly supported slavery by buying products made using slave labor.

WHOLESALE AND RETAIL
FREE LABOR WAREHOUSE.
GEO. W. TAYLOR,
N. W. cor. of Fifth and Cherry Streets,
PHILADELPHIA.
MANUFACTURER AND VENDOR
OF FREE LABOR DRY GOODS.
FREE LABOR GROCERIES FOR SALE.

A Philadelphia merchant advertises slave-free labor products available in his warehouse. COURTESY LIBRARY COMPANY OF PHILADELPHIA

Mrs. Jennings and her daughters worked tirelessly to make sure local church fairs were able to offer free labor products. They collected used clothing for needy black schoolchildren and circulated petitions to abolish slavery. Elizabeth's sister Matilda helped run sewing circles that spread the word on anti-slavery and created free labor merchandise. Products such as pincushions, bookmarks, and jewelry were all stamped with anti-slavery slogans and images.

An event to benefit the *Colored American* newspaper and mark the Ladies Literary Society's third anniversary was a showcase for the Jennings family as well. Male abolitionists were invited to partake in this "mental feast." The *Colored American* reported in its September 23, 1837, issue that the celebration "was conducted with the greatest propriety and elegance."

The "Order of Exercises" that August day called for "original composition, oratory, dialogues on temperance." Of the sixteen items listed in the program, four were performed by "Miss Jennings." Her first performance was a conversation with four other females called "First Appearance in Company" where they dressed as soldiers in the war on slavery. The next was a speech, "On the Improvement of the Mind," followed by a musical

Designed by Josiah Wedgwood in 1788, this medallion became a symbol of the anti-slavery movement while helping to raise funds as well.
COURTESY WEDGWOOD MUSEUM

rendition of "There's Nothing True but Heaven." Finally, Miss Jennings closed out the festivities with a "Poetic Address."

"On the Improvement of the Mind" stirred the crowd and so impressed the editors of the *Colored American* that it was reprinted in its entirety. The five-minute speech is part plea to rise up to improve and part call to fight for social change. Recognizing that "now is a momentous time," Miss Jennings demanded her audience take advantage of the opportunity.

However, she understood that the dark cloud of racism led to despair, self-neglect, and hopelessness. "Neglect will plunge us into deeper degradation," she predicted, "and keep us groveling in the dust, while our enemies will rejoice." Miss Jennings then issued a series of challenges. "Shall we bring this reproach on ourselves?" she asked. "Why sleep thus?" In short, she called on New York's black females to take control of their destiny.

Miss Jennings finished with a rousing cry for her community to seek "those gems for which we have united ourselves" and to always strive for perfection, which favors no color or cultural boundaries.

Historians differ on which Miss Jennings participated in that day's program. Some assume that it was Elizabeth who delivered the address rather than her mother. She is often credited as the author and speaker. As proof, they offer the newspaper's reference to "Miss Jennings" as the performer being an unmarried female. However, the newspaper appears to have used "Miss" when referring to any female, married or not, as was the custom at the time.

At the age of ten, it seems doubtful Elizabeth would have been called upon to deliver such a powerful recruitment message.

For the Jennings family, there were other outcomes from participating in anti-slavery activities. During 1838, the two Jennings sons were married within months of each other. Thomas Jr. married Sarah C. Cannard of Gardiner, Maine, while William wed New Englander Maria B. Smith. The following year, Sarah Jennings wed Samuel A. Smyth of Philadelphia. In February 1841, Matilda Jennings married James Thompson.

Located on the Kennebec River, Gardiner was known for exporting ice and paper and helping slaves north to freedom. Soon both of the Jennings brothers' wives were expecting. That year, Thomas Jr. left Gardiner on a mysterious trip to New Orleans via Cincinnati, Ohio.

The Jennings family was delighted that the next generation was on its way. However, this happiness was short-lived. On May 7, 1839, Thomas D. Jennings was born, but there was no joy. Sarah died from complications with the birth. Later, the boy followed. Both were buried in the rural cemetery in Gardiner. Elizabeth's brother Thomas was missing for months. With no forwarding address or way to contact him, Thomas Jr. was unaware his wife and child were gone. Now the family feared for his safety. Slave catchers may have seized him on the way to New Orleans or done worse. All they could do was wait and hope.

In April 1840, Maria and her infant died suddenly from tuberculosis. Ill from the disease himself, William passed away that fall on a journey to receive treatment in a warmer climate. The abolitionist movement lost one of its bright young stars.

Friend and fellow civil rights activist William C. Nell noted the "loss of our brother" in the *Liberator*. For a month, African American men in Boston and New York wore black armbands in William's honor. Grief shouted from the pages of the *Colored American*: "The good die first . . . his business did not alienate him from the cause of liberty . . . His devotion to the interests of the slave, and his suffering people is well known . . . Friend of my youth: Brother. Farewell!"

Others carried on in William's stead. As the *Colored American* predicted, the Ladies Literary Society of New York City "set an example for a rising generation." The seeds of freedom were planted for the next band of sisters to lead New York's black community. These young women took up the cause their mothers fought so hard for and made it their own. Elizabeth Jennings, Sarah Mapps Douglass, Sarah Forten, Maria Stewart, and Cordelia Ray all would continue a lifetime commitment to activist service.

By the late 1830s, confrontations between abolitionists and pro-slavery forces grew violent. To protect their African American friends, the white women would interlock arms with their black sisters and walk two by two through angry mobs blocking their way to meetings.

They were equals now, sisters in a struggle for common rights that would stretch into the twenty-first century. Elizabeth grew up with role

models from the Ladies Literary Society. The pride and self-confidence she learned from them would serve her well in the troubling years ahead.

"On the Improvement of the Mind" Was It Elizabeth or Mrs. Jennings?

In August 1837, the Ladies Literary Society of New York celebrated its third anniversary with a fund-raising event for the *Colored American* newspaper. A group of male abolitionists—Elizabeth's father among them—attended the festivities and donated money to the cause.

"On the Improvement of the Mind" was the seventh act in the program. Miss Jennings was listed as the orator. Was it young Elizabeth Jennings who delivered the speech, or her mother? History makes it difficult to discern. Below is the text of the address that was reprinted in the September 23, 1837, issue of the *Colored American*.

Friends, in appearing before you this evening, I find words inadequate to express my feelings, for the honor conferred on me of addressing you, in celebration of this anniversary. I am conscious of my incapacity to do justice to the task allotted me. But as our object is improvement, and feeling that yours is the same, we have but to solicit your kind indulgence.

It is now a momentous time, a time that calls us to exert all our powers, and among the man of them, the mind is the greatest, and great care should be taken to improve it with diligence. We should cultivate those powers and dispositions of the mind, which may prove advantageous to us. It is impossible to attain to the sphere for which we were created, without persevering. It is certain we were formed for society, and it is our duty and interest to cultivate social qualities and dispositions—to endeavor to make ourselves useful and pleasing to others, to promote and encourage their happiness—to cherish the friendly affections, that we may find in them the source of the greatest blessings this world can afford.

(continued)

But, alas! Society too often exhibits a far different scene, and this is in consequence of neglect of cultivation, which certainly is much more fatal than we can imagine. Neglect will plunge us into deeper degradation, and keep us groveling in the dust, while our enemies will rejoice and say, we do not believe they [colored people] have any minds; if they have, they are unsusceptible of improvement. My sisters, allow me to ask the question, shall we bring this reproach on ourselves? Doubtless you answer NO, we will strive to avoid it. But hark! Methinks I hear the well-known voice of Abigail M. Matthews, saying you can avoid it. Why sleep thus? Awake and slumber no more—arise, put on your armor, ye daughters of America, and start forth in the full field of improvement. You can all do some good, and if you do but little it will increase in time. The mind is powerful, and by its efforts your influence may be as near perfection, as that of those which have extended over kingdoms, and is applauded by thousands.

Let us accord with that voice which we hear urging us and resolve to adorn our minds with a more abundant supply of those gems for which we have united ourselves—nor let us ever think any occasion too trifling for our best endeavors. It is by constant aiming at perfection in everything that we may at length attain to it.

Chapter VI

Zack Comes to Town

But since you wish to hear my part, And urge me to begin it. I'll strive for praise, with all my heart, Though small the hope to win it.

—Thaddeus Mason Harris,
"The Little Orator"

A FRIGHTENED EIGHT-YEAR-OLD WAITED NERVOUSLY AS HIS SCHOOLMATES filed out of the church basement with hushed concern. Unable to complete his assignment that day, the boy was asked to remain after class by the principal. In the 1840s, every child knew that discipline was harsh and painful. The tiny boy trembled as the twenty-one-year-old headmaster towered over him asking why his work wasn't completed. Stammering, he said he couldn't write or recite poetry very well.

Fully awaiting physical pain, the child was surprised when the young teacher bent down and began to write out a poem for him. "Will you try and learn this for me?" the principal gently asked. The boy promised to do his best. The next day, he recited "The Little Orator" to the cheers of his fellow students, teachers, and parents. Although written some forty years earlier by Thaddeus Mason Harris for a four-year-old prodigy named Edward Everett, the poem and the lesson it taught him stayed with Asa Stillman the rest of his life.

Stillman went on to become a prominent doctor in upstate New York and retold this story to various newspapers thirty years later when his principal became the twenty-first president of the United States. The incident made such an impression on Asa that years before Arthur became president he named his first son Chester Arthur Stillman. The ability to turn conflict toward compassion and enemies to friends would serve Arthur well throughout his lifetime.

The fifteen-year-old Chester must have been as intimidated by his surroundings as Stillman was of public speaking as he approached the doors of the Lyceum and Academy building for the first time in 1844. Schenectady was a far cry from the idyllic meadows and brooks of Whipple City. The Elder Arthur became a minister for the First Baptist Church in what is now Watervliet, New York, for a salary increase, but he was after much more. The Lyceum had strong connections to nearby Union College, as did the primary school principal from Union Village. The greater Albany area had all the educational resources the Elder Arthur envisioned for his son.

The Lyceum was an oddity unto itself. A kind of nineteenth-century Google campus, it was hailed as futuristic during its time. It was a massive, two-story, octagon-shaped structure constructed of rough-cut brick covered with stucco to appear as if it was black granite. Each corner of the octagon had a battlement topped off with quatrefoil pinnacles that spiraled into the sky, with a turret in the center of the building fronted by two smaller chapels lined with stained glass windows and parapets. It looked like a medieval castle rising from the corner of Yates and Union Streets.

The interior was no less strange. The main floor was reserved for wealthy students learning the classics in the "male department," what might be considered high school today. The basement was used for primary education. The second floor served as a lecture hall that held up to 150 people for community meetings. For students, those seats and desks were placed in three-sided boxes much like smaller office cubicles. However, the seats were turned toward one of the eight octagon walls, not the teacher. This allowed the instructor at the raised lectern in the center of the room to survey the masses for miscreants and nodding-off pupils without their knowledge. The concept behind the unusual seating arrangement was to free young minds of distractions so these schoolboys would be open to listening intently to their instructor's every word. Judging by the holes reported to have been gouged into the cubicle walls, it appeared to have had the opposite effect. Spitballs and notes were exchanged on a much more accelerated basis than any lecture ideas were.

An 1842 advertisement for the school in the *Schenectady City Directory* showed the academic schedule Chet was put through. Courses were offered in higher English, Latin, and Greek for $5 a quarter or $7.50 a term. Common English rang up a bill of $3.50 a quarter. Stationary classes were a mere 50 cents ($1 from 1844 would be worth more than $35 today).

Chet fit right in with all the city slickers from Schenectady. Just as his father did, he took a classical route to education, enrolling in Latin, English, and philosophy classes. Early on in his freshman year, Chet joined the school newspaper, *The Lyceum Review*, as a coeditor. Each edition was stockpiled with items of campus interest, student poetry, and musings of the day.

Little from this period in Chet's life was saved. One item of interest that seems to foreshadow events remains. It's a short essay called "The Influence of the Press"—an unusual topic for a fifteen-year-old who grew up in rural communities his whole life where newspapers were mostly gossip and social events. At approximately five hundred words, the piece not only demonstrates the youngster's rhetorical skills and worldly knowledge but also illuminates the influences on his life and how words can haunt long after they are written. It has the cadence and style of a sermon, with many dashes and commas for pauses and words underlined for emphasis.

Chet opens his essay strongly, stating that nations shouldn't be judged on their territorial size or wealth, but rather on "the superiority of *virtue* and *intellect*" of its people, who are "the best standing army that can be set for the defense of liberty."

From there he sets to his main thesis:

> *What a powerful auxiliary to a nation's prosperity is the press. In no part of the globe is it so powerful,—so omnipotent in its action, so omnipresent in its influence, as in the United States. It speaks to every one—making itself felt in every public department of State, as well as in the walks of private life. If all its energies emanated from proper principles—if were the zeal which directs its efforts, a zeal for man's intellectual and moral good; the press in America, from its increased power, might in a very short time, undo much of the mischief, which its vicious direction has entailed on the country.*

He then lashes into the press as "conductors of our periodicals write *to please* and print *for pay*" before asking a question that is still asked today.

> *A lying press, is as bad as a lying tongue, and commonly, does more mischief. What must other nations think of the wisdom, and integrity of those men elevated to the highest offices in the gift of a free people, if they take for truth the representations given of them by their political opponents.*

That fall, Chet also received his first lesson in politics. With the 1844 presidential election pitting Whig Party candidate Henry Clay against Democrat James Polk looming, people hoisted poles for their supporters to gather around and discuss politics. A native of Kentucky, Clay was represented by an "ash pole," while Polk supporters raised a "hickory pole" to boost their candidate. Two such poles were raised at the Lyceum school grounds, with Chet falling into the Clay camp. After some name-calling and shouting, a schoolyard brawl between the two sides ensued. Polk won the election, but Chet got a taste of his first political fight mixed with a little blood, sweat, and tears.

Recalling the incident thirty-six years later, he quipped to the *Boston Herald*, "I have been in many a political battle since then, but none livelier, or that more thoroughly enlisted me."

In the fall of 1845, Chet was accepted into Union College as a sophomore, a testament to his homeschooling and standing at the Lyceum and Academy. While Elizabeth Jennings and her family fought repression from society through education, Chet found personal liberation in learning. In many ways, Union was the ideal school for him. It was led since 1804 by Dr. Eliphalet Nott, who secured 250 acres of land in Schenectady to make the Union campus a rival of Harvard, Yale, and Princeton. Seventy-two at the time, Nott had more than thirty patents to his name and rode about campus in a custom-made three-wheeled cart. Physically abused himself, Nott didn't believe in harsh physical punishments. Instead, he sought to show that morality could motivate behavior on its own, and his students loved him for it, calling him "Old Prex." ("Prex" or "prexy" was an eighteenth-century slang term for college president rarely used by Arthur's time.) Because Nott was also willing to give a young man a second chance, the school earned the nickname "Botany Bay" after the penal colony established in Australia.

Chet helped it live up to that handle. Freed from the intense glare of his father's moralist teaching, Arthur became something of a cutup and prankster at Union. He also joined the Psi Upsilon fraternity and began to get a taste for the finer things in life that his austere upbringing didn't permit. Frat boy Chet was fined more than once for skipping morning prayer services and breaking school property during various mischievous escapades. He carved his initials in the woodwork of several buildings. Among his more notable pranks was throwing the West College bell into the Erie Canal, preventing classes from starting.

At the same time, the young man had a serious and sentimental side. With science, engineering, and surveying catching the imagination of the industrializing country, Chet kept at least two notebooks of inspiring quotes, one filled with the verse of English poets, the other containing Latin quotations.

One of his first college papers, from September 1845, was a whimsical tale called "A brief Universal history from the Deluge to the present time." It's the kind of essay someone who wants to be noticed writes. He combines both ancient religious history and American history into one short paper.

> *Lord Cornwallis, and his forces then came up with the American army in the great Desert, and put them to flight, Washington being deprived of life by a spent cannon ball. The prophet Miller upon receipt of this intelligence, started in pursuit of Cornwallis at the head of the united forces of the Abolitionists and Mormons and finding him at Saratoga Springs, rescued him to ad absurdum.*

As the content of this essay shows, the Elder Arthur still cast a long shadow on his son. But their relationship was by no means adversarial. The year Chet started at Union, Nott awarded Elder Arthur with an honorary master of arts degree. Following his literary urges, Elder Arthur began a four-year stint editing what we would call a supermarket tabloid, the *Antiquarian and General Review*. It was the *National Enquirer* of its day, featuring articles about a 370-year-old man, children taming fish, and the discovery of salt. Even Dr. Nott wrote articles for the tabloid. The review also featured writing from a relatively new genre called the short story.

"The Defaulter—A True Tale" was a Poe-like saga about a guilt-ridden wife driven to suicide written by CAA, the editor's son.

Father and son collaborated on multiple creative projects together. Elder Arthur allowed his son to find his own way despite being close at hand.

Chet became president of the Delphian Institute, the college debating team, in 1847, vowing to his fellow classmates in a speech to "discharge the duties of my office, inexperienced as I am in parliamentary rules." He taught at a local school during recesses to help pay his tuition. Beginning to view the world beyond his small-town life, Chet saw his father's disgust of slavery in a broader context.

Among his few surviving papers is a strong condemnation of slavery he wrote before graduation from Union. In it he describes "the disastrous effects of slavery":

> *Such a political pestilence having spread itself over the South, every southern breeze bears to the North the seeds of this ruinous disease and political death follows in its wake. The mild northern breezes coming in contact with the putrefied air of the South are soon tainted, & the whole vast continent bids fair to fall under the blighting effects.*

By all accounts, Chet was popular with his classmates. At age twenty-one, he was six feet two inches tall and athletic-looking with dark eyes and wore a fashionable moustache. Chet Arthur, they might say in the nineteenth-century vernacular, commanded a "physical system that was finely formed." A college fraternity brother, William P. Chambers, put it another way: He was "slender and graceful in form, a face beaming with intelligence, and often wearing a winning smile."

However, he wasn't overly obsessed with the opposite sex and expressed fear to his sisters that he might spend his life as a bachelor. He was loyal to friends and would go out of his way to show appreciation. William E. Robinson recalled a whistle stop at the Schenectady Railroad Station when Chet arrived to greet him with a number of his fraternity brothers. "After a few minutes pleasant conversation, the train moved on and the parting cheers with which they saluted me are still ringing in my ears."

Chet also had his inner circle of close associates, those chosen few who felt comfortable expressing their deepest fears and desires to one another. For Chet, those confidants were Campbell Allen and James Masten.

Together they were the Three Musketeers, enjoying each other's company while laughing at their own inane jokes and ridiculous remarks. While Chet was visiting his morose younger sister Malvina during the winter of 1853, she returned from a neighbor to write this in her diary: "Came home again and found here Chester, Campbell, and Mr. Masten, and just now they are having considerable fun trying to make the table tip by magnetizing it."

They even came up with their own nicknames for each other. Campbell was "John," and Chet was "Zack." James was marrying Chet's sister Almeda, so that was his identity. Chet's letters to his friends reveal an idealistic young man feeling his way in the world. As Zack, he could be the passionate dreamer who lived for the moment and developed what would become an Arthur trademark—late night chats about ambitious plans.

Chet looked forward to and lived for these encounters. As he wrote to "John," who was ill at the time, "What a life we did lead last winter! You and I particularly—sitting up like owls till two or three in the morning with our pipes, over a warm fire—quite satisfied with our little world within."

In 1848, Chet graduated from Union College seventeenth out of a class of seventy-nine and gave a speech at graduation on "The Destiny of Genius." Chet's immediate path was to complete the legal training his father was never able to. He wanted to be a full-fledged lawyer.

The recently opened State and National Law School in nearby Ballston Spa, New York, offered him the best opportunity for a legal education. Chet was accepted in 1852, but an African American applicant, John Mercer Langston, was denied entrance two years prior. Because Langston was light-skinned, the trustees would accept him if he would renounce his race. He wouldn't, and studied law privately in Ohio to become the second African American in the United States to pass the bar exam. He also served in the US House of Representatives and as the first dean of Howard University's law school. His great-nephew was Langston Hughes.

At the cost of thirty dollars a term paid in advance, Chet needed first to support himself. He worked as a teacher for fifteen dollars a month between his school semesters. While spot preaching, the Elder Arthur found him a job as the principal of the basement academy in North Pownal, Vermont, where he mentored Stillman and his classmates. Three years later, a penmanship teacher and future president, James Garfield, joined the academy staff. By then Arthur had left North Pownal for a better-paying position. The two schoolteachers never met back then, but their destinies were tied together as presidential running mates on the 1880 Republican ticket.

Now making thirty-five dollars a month as principal of a school in Cohoes, New York, Chet was able to save enough money to consider an internship at a law firm to complete his legal education. These were good times for Zack and friends; the dreaming was always better than the doing. Cohoes was a tough, hard-bitten town ten miles north of the state capital in Albany. It was known as "Spindle City" because of all the textile factories needed to weave slave-picked cotton from the south. Chet knew from Malvina, who also taught at the school, that the students there were less than enthusiastic learners. After four other teachers quit the position, he realized it was either them or him. He was challenged right away by three teenage troublemakers. Chet certainly possessed the physical prowess to punish the students, but instead, one by one he made them leave the room and placed them in classes for younger children. At the end of the day, he called the three together and told them to come back as good students. They did.

Being around his family was a constant reminder to Chet that even as adults the friction between "Pa Arthur" and his siblings was all-consuming. Malvina, who was let go from her teaching job in Cohoes, still clung to Chet for protection from their father's fury. In her diary from 1853, she wrote: "I could find it very pleasant here at home, if it were not for that one, great hindrance." Her only consolation was the presence of Chester, "but perhaps I shall find it more lonely when Chester goes away." Soon her brother left briefly and Malvina was compelled to confront her father's reproach. On July 11 she wrote, "Ma's so sick. Mr. Loomis'[s] been here to call, and Pa's remarks completely unstrung my nerves. I'm just down sick. I wish Chester were home." Five days later she lamented, "Chester went off to Cohoes, and left me alone again."

The other Arthur children didn't fare much better. The oldest child, Regina, was widowed at a young age, while Annie (the fourth) suffered from chronic mental health issues. William Jr. was severely debilitated in a battle during the Civil War. Malvina died alone and incoherent. Jane and George died young from illness. Sisters Mary and Almeda appeared to live normal, happy lives. To get away from his family, Chet needed the law. It was his ticket away from all the Arthurs. This is not to say that he didn't get along with his siblings. As Malvina's diary shows, the Arthurs cared for each other a great deal, but Chet needed his space.

By 1850, Erastus Dean Culver moved his abolitionist fight to the battleground of New York City. He opened the law office of Culver & Parker with his mentor Judge William H. Parker. The firm specialized in defending innocent blacks from the Fugitive Slave Act. Some thought Culver secretly helped slaves out of the city through the Underground Railroad. One can imagine the eager student Chet listening to Culver's tales of political intrigue and bustling city life and wanting to be part of it. He was in love with Manhattan before ever visiting it, and Culver needed help with his growing law practice.

The State and National Law School was almost as interesting a place to take classes as the Lyceum was. Built in 1803 as the Sans Souci Hotel, the building was humongous. It had 180 rooms and accommodated 300 guests, among them James Fenimore Cooper, Andrew Jackson, and Washington Irving. As Ballston Spa's mineral waters declined, so did the hotel's profits.

The inordinate amount of space allowed the school trustees to try innovative, hands-on learning techniques recreating mock courtrooms complete with witnesses, bailiffs, lawyers, and judges. For a startup, it had an impressive roster of guest lecturers: Henry Clay, Horace Greeley, and former presidents Martin Van Buren and John Tyler. Even with scrimping and saving, Chet couldn't come up with enough money to finish law school. Despite all his efforts, he was still in the same position his father was. With the law school moving to Poughkeepsie, New York, Chet decided it was time for him to make a move too.

Chet must have thought the world seemed to be shrinking as the steamer chugged down the North River closer and closer to Manhattan Island. The familiar Catskill Mountains, the fortress of West Point, and soaring Palisades gave way to a terrain of brush. Ships darted and dodged in near misses, blowing their horns and ringing their bells. On the Jersey side a vast, open green field played host to a ball-hitting game that drew hundreds of witnesses.

An 1859 daguerreotype of a crusading lawyer. Arthur's work on the Lemmon appeal was critical to its being upheld and launched his career in backroom politics. COURTESY NATIONAL PORTRAIT GALLERY

The Empire City spread endlessly before Chester. Row upon row of brick buildings and warehouses piled below the ethereal spires of the Trinity, St. Paul's, and St. John's churches. Before them, a forest of ship masts surrounded the city like an ancient castle moat. Chester surely imagined the dazzling nightlife that awaited him—fast-moving carriages whisking him and his new associates nightly to theaters and fine restaurants.

He began his yearlong apprenticeship as a law clerk for Culver & Parker about the same time Elizabeth Jennings returned to teach at School No. 2 of the New York Society for the Promotion of Education among Colored Children. Elizabeth made an annual salary of $225. Elizabeth was highly thought of and acted as vice principal.

Arthur's first impressions of Manhattan were not of a thriving and alluring metropolis. Without his school chums to talk to, the idealistic Zack found he was lonely and that a law clerk's tasks were repetitive. He wrote home about the dreariness of legal research and occasionally went out to the theater. He wrote his mother that most of his days were spent working from eight in the morning to six at night at a "variety of delightful duties at the office." As was the custom for single men, he lived in a boardinghouse, not unlike the ones Elizabeth's father operated.

At the Bancroft House, Chester took his meals and spent his free time conversing with other residents, playing cards, or singing in the parlor. It was a transient lifestyle. People were always coming and going with no sense of family. However, the city did provide seasonal distractions to look forward to. The first of May in New York City, when all leases expired, was known as "May Day" or "Moving Day." It was akin to a free vaudeville act full of laughs and surprises. Cartmen willing to lift any trunk during the year suddenly developed the airs of royalty, charging whatever fee fancied them.

By seven in the morning, the entire city was on the move; mattresses went out windows, sofas made their way down stairs, and pianos dangled from ropes over sidewalks. Perilous piles of movables crammed the streets as people crawled all over alleys and doorways like ants on a scrap of pie. The first mishap might come from a wife carrying dishes or a mule bucking a wagon. Whatever the mischief, the calamity reverberated throughout the city as people shouted, "Stand from under!" over and over again, as shoes, books, chairs, and linens rained down on unsuspecting pedestrians.

Life in New York City didn't seem any more exciting than home for the shy and forlorn Zack. A particularly brutal winter must have added to the stark desolation the young man probably felt living alone in the large city. Eventually Chet struck up a lasting friendship with his boardinghouse roommate Henry Gardiner, a young lawyer with ambition. Otherwise he kept to himself.

That spring all the hard work paid off. In May 1854, Zack the rambunctious student passed the bar exam and became Chester Alan Arthur, Esquire. Now a full-fledged lawyer, his name was added to the firm's door at 289 Broadway—Culver, Parker & Arthur.

The poverty-stricken student from upstate New York had arrived. Always striving to please his demanding father, Zack was ready to fulfill his promise. Similar to the Little Orator in the poem he had his student memorize, praise wouldn't come easily. In the months to come, the paths of the two young schoolteachers whose backgrounds were so similar yet separated by the distance of race would cross.

CHAPTER VII

City of Omnibuses

Horsecars where the courtesies of life are impossible, and the inherent dignity of a person is denied.

—WILLIAM DEANS HOWELLS,
SUBURBAN SKETCHES

Elizabeth Jennings might not have known who Blaise Pascal was, but he had an enormous impact on her life.

Born in Clermont-Ferrand, France, in 1623, Pascal was truly a Renaissance man. A child prodigy, he created early calculating machines, developed mathematical theories, and was a philosopher as well as a renowned physical scientist (Pascal's law). Late in life, he convinced a cadre of French noblemen to provide financing for a transportation service that could be used to travel about Paris to preset destinations. To seal the deal, he got the Sun King, Louis XIV, to grant his venture a royal monopoly.

This five-penny transit system started in 1662 with seven horse-drawn *voitures*, or carriages, running along regular routes. Each coach could carry six to eight passengers. Pascal's new public transit vehicles would become known as omnibuses, from the Latin phrase *Justitia Omnibus*, meaning "justice for all." In Pascal's world transportation *for all* meant only for the nobility. Pascal's bus routes lived on for a dozen years after his death before the upper class lost interest in public transit.

Pascal's idea was before its time. By the early nineteenth century, omnibus systems quickly sprang up in London, Paris, Boston, Philadelphia, and New York. Despite concerns that mixing classes of people would cause social problems, anyone requesting to ride on an omnibus was allowed to pay his or her way onboard. Omnibuses that began to reappear during the 1820s cost as much as 12 to 25 cents per passenger, well beyond the means of common laborers.

These early omnibuses were little more than glorified stagecoaches. They were heavy, cumbersome vehicles whose wheels mired in mud or broke in holes. Usually pulled by four horses, an omnibus carried between twelve to twenty-eight passengers, with more people piled on the roof or hanging off the back. The buses swung from side to side and were operated at a top speed of four miles an hour.

Omnibuses were short on comfort too. Steps up into the car were high and hard to get to and the seats unforgiving. Unheated, these open-air vehicles relied on straw thrown on the floor to provide warmth (losing one's fare in that hay was a common ruse used to get a free pass onboard). There were no traffic signals or road instructions. Buggies, wagons, pedestrians, and livestock all headed in their own direction at their own speed. Everything merged in a beehive of crawling, wiggling transportation on narrow city streets.

On the best of days, taking an omnibus was a mixed bag. An omnibus line was a relatively inexpensive business to start. In the 1830s, New York City began granting licenses to private investors to develop omnibus services. This mode of transportation was going nowhere until the concept of rail tracks was adapted for street use. Through the laying down of tracks sheathed in iron, metal wheels carrying heavier passenger loads could be guided along predetermined railed routes.

It took an immigrant New Yorker to adapt these early coaches into the first horse-drawn streetcars. Though his father was British and his mother Scottish, John Stephenson was born in County Armagh, Ireland, in 1809. He came to Manhattan with his family at the age of two. As a youngster attending New York City's public schools, Stephenson spent his spare time building toy wagons, sleighs, and birdcages.

At sixteen, he attended Wesleyan Seminary in Manhattan to fulfill his father's wish of a mercantile career. But Stephenson had another calling. After three years of pleading, his father gave in and allowed the boy to pursue his dream of becoming a coach maker. After an apprenticeship on Broome Street, Stephenson was offered a small repair shop by livery owner Abram Brower at 667 Broadway. There he set to work repairing coaches for Brower, who operated omnibuses on Broadway.

Within a year, the shop Stephenson started with four hundred dollars had grown another twelve hundred dollars in value. Stephenson wasn't satisfied with repairing other people's coaches. He wanted to design better, more efficient models that served the needs of New York's growing industrial class. Stephenson began experimenting with coaches and for a good reason. The fledgling New York and Harlem Railroad Company was planning a route from Prince to Fourteenth Street. It was the first streetcar charter to be granted in the United States.

The new railway company put out a request for "a specimen car" from various coach makers, including Stephenson. The brainchild of the company's president, John Mason, this was to be the first railway in the country to use horse-drawn cars on iron tracks. He was also the founder of Chemical Bank. His daughter Mary was Edith Wharton's great-aunt and the inspiration for Mrs. Manson Mingott in the novel *The Age of Innocence*. Mason chose an east-side route for his rail system, convinced that land-based transport could never compete with the west-side steamships of the North River (the Hudson River).

Shoppers, pedestrians, and real estate moguls had their street terminology. One always wanted to be dropped off by an omnibus on the "dollar side" of an avenue or thoroughfare. Going north, this was the left-hand side of the street, where the high-end and more profitable retailers were. The right-hand side, or "shilling side," was for cheap dry goods shops. Businesses paid higher rents for dollar-side storefronts that coincidently matched Mason's concerns. The Hudson River is on the left going northbound, the East River on the right. (Today the values have flipflopped. The east side of Manhattan has been generally more well-to-do than the west.)

In this environment, Stephenson set to work on his new horsecar. Tragedy stuck in the spring of 1832 as the prototype neared completion. A fire destroyed Bower's livery stables and Stephenson's shop. Undeterred, he quickly relocated his business to Elizabeth Street and continued to work on his new horsecar. It consisted of three separate compartments seating ten passengers each. He then dropped the vehicle's floor between the wheels and added elliptical springs to improve riding comfort.

The driver sat on the roof and used a foot brake while patrons entered from side doors and the back, making it easier to board quickly. The vehicle has been aptly described as "a cross between an omnibus, a rockaway, and an English railway coach," according to an eyewitness at its unveiling. (A rockaway was a light, roofed stagecoach.) Stephenson knew who he worked for. Confident it would perform admirably, Stephenson named his prototype the "John Mason." His other early horsecars received nicknames such as "President," "Mentor," and "Forget-Me-Not."

These early cars, built for the working class, were ornate, featuring glass windows, latticework, and reversible cushioned seats as well as stovepipe heating throughout. The *Rochester Daily Democrat* called the Stephenson horsecar a "traveling palace . . . gorgeously flowered and varnished."

The mile-long Harlem railway opened on November 26, 1832, to more bemused onlookers than awestruck consumers awaiting the arrival of public transportation. The usual political suspects such as the mayor, city council members, and guests were present. According to transit historian W.H. Brown, railroad officials were aware of public concerns about the ability of horsecars to stop to avoid accidents.

According to *Wonders and Curiosities of the Railway*, by William Sloane Kennedy, an impromptu safety demonstration was hastily arranged by the company vice president. The staging was near the corner of Bowery and Bond Streets using the flagship vehicle the "John Mason" and another horsecar. When the vice president signaled for both horsecars to stop, the experienced driver of the John Mason deftly applied his brake to come to a halt. However, the operator of the second car grabbed the reins to his horses instead of using the brake, causing the streetcars to collide. On impact, the frightened political officials scattered like rats from a watchman's lamp, triggering a comic uproar from the crowd.

While no one was hurt, the histrionics of the railroad executive were imitated on the streets to laughter for days afterward. It was the first streetcar collision in Manhattan. So began nearly two hundred years of public skepticism about transit officials. Damaged but intact, the "John Mason" completed its maiden journey to Fourteenth Street. While some egos and fenders were dented, Stephenson's reputation grew exponentially.

In April 1833, he received a US patent for his design of the "John Mason" signed by President Andrew Jackson. Like Elizabeth's father, who also earned a patent, he proudly displayed it throughout his life. In all, Stephenson was issued or assigned at least eighteen patents. Orders for his omnibuses and horsecars came in from around the world. Brooklyn; Paterson, New Jersey; Florida; and Cuba all wanted his streetcars.

These vehicles were so numerous on city streets that one observer noted, "The white tops of the omnibuses resemble the waves of the ocean . . . we might walk from one end of Broadway to the other upon them." As the *Gazette and General Advertiser* exclaimed that year, New York was becoming a "City of Omnibuses."

Within three years, John Stephenson opened an expanded factory in Harlem. By 1845, his business relocated to Twenty-Seventh Street and Fourth Avenue (now Park), where the six-story structure took up sixteen city lots. What was once a curiosity became a driver of the city's economy.

Stephenson knew that to stay on top he needed to constantly improve his product. With a horsecar, there were only two ways to significantly impact costs: lighten the load and reduce the number of horses needed per car. Doing one led to reducing the other. By switching from oak to hickory (a lighter wood) for his cabs, and adding more glass windows, he slashed the weight of his vehicles. His original car was 6,800 pounds; Stephenson's improved design was only half that weight. That reduced the number of horses needed to pull the car from four to two.

He eliminated the side doors and added a single entrance at the back of the car. Seats were placed along the sides of the bus. He invented a bell pulley so passengers could ring when they wanted to exit. He also claimed to have invented the rearview mirror so drivers could glance behind themselves without turning their heads from the road. Stephenson lost this patent when the judge said he was trying to lay claim to common sense.

The success of Stephenson's streetcars didn't translate into more riders on Manhattan's rails. Although the Fourth Avenue line eventually expanded from Fourteenth Street up into Harlem, it was considered a failure. In Stephenson's 1893 obituary, the *New York Times* opined that the Harlem line's lack of success was "owing perhaps to local prejudice."

Public transportation was as much a social experiment as it was a feat of engineering and technology. Mixing classes of people, nationalities, and sexes was a rare occurrence at a time when meetings that allowed men and women to freely intermingle were called "promiscuous." The concept of free men or women of different races being treated on equal footing and traveling together wasn't on the table. Manhattan's rail companies all banned African Americans from riding with white customers. Some occasionally ran "colored only" cars or allowed blacks to occupy outer platforms. These companies believed Manhattan's white community just wasn't ready for the "mass" in mass transportation.

Stephenson had problems too. The financial crisis of the late 1830s left him in dire straits. Bonds accepted instead of cash left him owing creditors for unfulfilled orders. He lost everything. As he did after the fire nearly a decade earlier, Stephenson started from scratch. Ignoring bankruptcy laws, he paid back every cent he owed creditors, earning the nickname "Honest John."

Resistance from omnibus and coach companies also contributed to the slow adaptation of streetcar transportation. Over time, New Yorkers may have seen streetcars as the lesser of two evils. Steam locomotives were a danger to pedestrians on the street. Boilers exploded, killing people. By 1844, the Common Council banned steam-powered rails below Thirty-Second Street, and then pushed the ban back to Forty-Second Street. No one wanted the unsightly rail tracks on their streets. Wherever they appeared, residents threatened to vandalize them.

All that would change in the 1850s with the opening of the Croton Reservoir and the Crystal Palace. As city life stretched north past the liveries of Longacre Square (Times Square), everyday working people needed to traverse more and more of Manhattan Island. In the early 1850s, the city moved quickly to develop its streetcar infrastructure.

In 1852, the Sixth Avenue Railroad Company became the first streetcar railway to be awarded a charter since the Fourth Avenue Harlem line began service twenty years earlier. Often these companies were also responsible for paving the roads when laying down their streetcar track. Horse-drawn railways operated on the Third, Fourth, Sixth, and Eighth Avenues while freewheeling coaches and omnibuses roamed the rest of the city.

The following year, the Third Avenue line began operation from City Hall to Sixty-Second Street. On Tenth Avenue, a street-level freight train ran that killed and mutilated so many people that the road was called "Death Avenue." Horsecar lines came later to Ninth and Second Avenues as well.

Everyone used these streetcar tracks interchangeably. Carriages, coaches, and omnibuses all tried to jump on the tracks and take advantage of the smoother ride. In its July 19, 1855, edition, the *Brooklyn Daily Eagle* reported just such an instance that had tragic results near City Hall on Fulton Street in Brooklyn. A wagon using streetcar rails was in the way of a Greenwood horsecar and wouldn't leave the tracks. A collision occurred, destroying the wagon and resulting in a finger being amputated from a five-year-old boy.

According to the *Brooklyn Eagle*, this was a common occurrence. "It is a wonder that such accidents as these are not more frequent, and some rule should be adopted and enforced whereby the probability of such occurrences would be avoided."

Then, as it is now, the cost of a ride was a major point of dispute. The city's Common Council allowed the railway companies to charge a nickel fare. However, many critics thought the railroads could still make a nice profit at 3 cents a head. Others complained that Manhattan was losing its population and tax base because the railroads didn't extend far enough uptown.

The lack of horsecar service on Second Avenue was blamed for killing off the economic progress of that area. The iron rails of these streetcar routes caused all sorts of problems for crosstown traffic by breaking wheels or wagons getting stuck in them. It's amazing that anyone ever got to where they were going.

Newspapers were unrelenting in their views of the transportation system. The *New York Herald* declared an omnibus ride "a perfect bedlam on wheels." The *Tribune* said these city horsecars were unsurpassed in their ability to "shoot passengers into the mud." The *New York Daily Times* reported that "incidents on the Third Avenue are so numerous since the railroad's inception that a single one is scarcely worth remembering."

Drivers too were known for their roughshod ways. In 1856, a "Great Indignation Meeting" was held at the Hotel De Mulligan to discuss all the "ills and 'oles" of Broadway, including the rudeness of streetcar drivers.

Even with these drawbacks, Manhattan's transit system expanded from 70 omnibuses in 1830 to 683 coaches carrying 120,000 passengers daily by 1854. That year omnibuses made about 13,400 trips a day across Manhattan on 27 routes. Five years after their inception, the new horsecars routes carried more than 23 million passengers.

As Manhattan's free African American community began to assert itself economically and politically in the years before the Civil War, public transportation would become the next battleground.

Chapter VIII

Late for Church

The heavy omnibus, the driver with his interrogating thumb, the clank of the shod horses on the granite floor.

—Walt Whitman,
"Song of Myself"

Eighteen fifty-four was a year of extremes in New York City. As noted in the *New York Daily Times*, "it was remarkable for wrecks, murders, swindles, defalcations, burnings on sea and land."

The year began with high hopes for a long-awaited railroad line on Broadway and ended with the arrests of several officials from the Harlem Railroad Company for stealing. By midyear, the first Cholera Hospital opened at 105 Franklin Street, not far from where Elizabeth taught. This was followed by another hospital opening on Mott Street, only to have the commissioners of health accused of suppressing data about cholera deaths as fear of an epidemic gripped Manhattan.

In a city of 515,000 residents, 500 children died the week of July 15—two-thirds were infants. Of the 817 New Yorkers to die, 12 were recorded as colored. About a mile or so uptown, Elizabeth Blackwell, the first woman in America to receive a medical degree, was busy establishing the New York Dispensary for Poor Women and Children by the newly rising tenements near Tompkins Square Park. At first, no one trusted a female doctor. But within two years, abolitionists such as William Lloyd Garrison helped her raise enough money to purchase the old Roosevelt home at 64 Bleecker Street and expand her services. (Today it's known as New York-Presbyterian/Lower Manhattan Hospital.)

In mid-July of 1854, a crippling heat wave suspended work in the shipyards. Sunstroke and "brain fever" caused dozens of deaths. Dead animals, horses mostly, were a problem. Their carcasses were left in the streets where they fell from heat exhaustion.

In 1854, there were 22,500 horses in Manhattan pulling streetcars, omnibuses, and coaches, according to Hilary J. Sweeney in the *American Journal of Irish Studies*. Decay, flies, and filth were everywhere, including an estimated two hundred tons of manure left daily on the streets.

The heat and stench must have affected Elizabeth Jennings's mood as she hastily readied for services on the morning of Sunday, July 16. As the organist for the First Colored American Congregational Church, it was important for her to arrive early and rehearse with the choir. She was leading her church's music program at a time when most organists and choir leaders were men.

She was running late, and temperatures were as high as ninety-eight degrees. In heavy Sunday-best garb, Elizabeth and Sarah Adams began their two-mile walk from Elizabeth's home at 167 Church Street. It was a wood-framed boardinghouse with a first-floor store and a slate roof, where she lived with her parents. Taking on boarders was a common practice in nineteenth-century New York, with about 30 percent of the population living in some 2,600 registered homes. Elizabeth's father was listed as the building's owner, where he ran his tailoring and dry-cleaning business. Also living there were two white families, those of Patrick Fitzgerald, a bricklayer, on one floor and W.S. Martin, a boatman, on another. The house had an open lot in the back used to grow vegetables, and a coal yard was located about a block away.

Across the road was the Mother African Methodist Episcopal Zion Church on the corner of Church and Franklin Streets. On the opposite corner was J.B. Purdy, a grocer in a mixed neighborhood of black and white residents. Living nearby were an upholsterer, laborer, teacher, and police captain. A block off Broadway, this was a well-to-do area with many brick-and-stone homes with large skylights. The Jennings's home was on the edge of this well-to-do area.

A section of the road before the Jennings's home was nicknamed the "Holy Ground" because of its many high-class brothels. While walking in the direction of the Third Avenue rail line, Elizabeth and Sarah headed for the streetcar stop. To reach the Third Avenue line, they turned right onto Pearl Street and hurried a few short blocks toward Chatham. To keep their dresses from dragging through the ever-present street offal and grime, in a ladylike fashion, they used a skirt lifter called a page or pulled on the chain of a chatelaine that raised the material from the soil without exposing the ankles.

A rendering of Chatham and Pearl Streets, where Elizabeth and her friend Sarah Adams tried to enter horsecar No. 6 to get to church on time. EMMET COLLECTION, NEW YORK PUBLIC LIBRARY

The two women made their way down Pearl Street and caught their breath at the corner of Chatham Street. There Elizabeth saw a horsecar in the distance slowly making its way uptown. She felt lucky that one was coming, she later explained in an interview with the *American Woman's Journal*. A rider could wait fifteen minutes or more for a bus on a Sunday. The light green car was sixteen feet long and could seat twenty-four passengers. It appeared half full as Elizabeth waved to flag the driver down. The deafening sound of the iron wheels scraping along the metal track as hooves stamped over stone suddenly ceased. Elizabeth swung herself up onto the high step-up platform in one motion. According to a reporter from the *American Woman's Journal*, while she waited for Sarah to join her, the conductor approached.

"You must wait for the next car," he said, pointing to the street.

"I am in a hurry and cannot wait for another car," she replied, moving toward the seats.

"But that car has your people in it," he added, motioning her back onto the boarding platform. "It is reserved for them."

"I have no people," exclaimed Elizabeth, becoming irritated. "This is no special occasion; I wish to go to church as I have been doing for the past six months and I do not wish to be detained."

The conductor would not let Elizabeth take a seat and asked her to leave the car. She again refused. The conductor demanded she wait in the street, but Elizabeth wouldn't budge.

"I will wait here on this platform until the other car arrives," she added, with a firmness in her voice that could only come from a schoolteacher.

An awkward silence drifted over the bus. People were used to travel delays—cows lying down on tracks, firefighters' hoses crossing their path, or a broken-down wagon blocking their progress. All these things were to be expected. The midday heat must have been unbearable, making the minutes seem more like hours. They waited in a standoff. Two African American women stood immovable on the platform, blocked from going any farther inside by an irascible white conductor.

Finally, the bus that seemed so far away was upon them. Elizabeth could see the sign in front that said Colored People Allowed in this Car.

"Is there room in your car?" Elizabeth shouted.

"No," the driver said, pulling up his horses. "There is more room in that car than there is in mine."

Elizabeth and Sarah thought that would be the end of it. Once again, they attempted to enter the streetcar, only to be prevented once more by the conductor. He stood in the doorway with his arms braced across the entrance. Unable to proceed, they simply stared back at him.

"I have as much time as you have and can wait as long," he said with a sneer on his face.

"Very well, we will see," Elizabeth snapped back.

One can imagine the collective groan from the bewildered riders as the saga continued with no end in sight. Even the horses, used to having a certain cadence to the day, must have begun to buck and crane their necks as if trying to see beyond their blinders. Growing impatient, the driver shouted at the conductor that he needed to move the bus. Now all eyes were on the conductor. Wiping the sweatband inside his cap, he threw his arms in the air.

"Well, you may go in," he barked at the women while taking their nickel fare. "But remember, if any of the passengers object, you shall go out, whether or not you want to, I'll put you out!"

That might have been the end of it for many people. Jennings was tired of being bullied. Tired of second-class treatment. Tired of having the color of her skin being used as an excuse for vile behavior.

"I am a respectable person," she snapped, admonishing the conductor. "Born and raised in New York and I have never been insulted before while going to church."

"I was born in Ireland, and I don't care where you were born!" exclaimed the agitated conductor. "You've got to come out of this car!"

Ever the educator, Elizabeth gave the Third Avenue conductor a lecture on equality that still rings true today.

"It makes no difference where a man was born; he's no better or worse for that, provided he behaves himself," she said, "but you are a good-for-nothing, impudent fellow, who insults genteel people on their way to church."

"I'll put you out of this car," he shouted.

"Don't you lay a hand on me," cried Elizabeth.

Suddenly turning, the conductor grabbed Jennings by the shoulders before she could sit and pushed her back toward the door. Elizabeth grabbed a window sash and held on for her life. Unable to remove her on his own, the conductor yelled for the driver to "fasten his horses" and assist him. Together they knocked Sarah back down the stairs. Turning to Jennings, the two men grabbed her by each arm, breaking her grip on the window. Then they dragged her out onto the platform to face a several-foot drop to the street.

"Murder, murder!" screamed Elizabeth.

"Stop, you'll kill her, don't kill her!" pleaded Sarah.

Elizabeth was tossed headfirst into the street as one might throw a bag of trash or old clothes. In a billow of dust, her face scraped against the filthy cobblestone road, leaving her bleeding, bruised, and dizzy from the fall. A part of her just wanted to lie there and cry. Her ribs hurt, her shoulder stung, and it was hard for her to see.

She got to her knees, stood, and began to limp away from the conductor. Then Jennings stopped and slowly turned around, wiping grime and blood from her face. She took two steps back toward the horsecar to pick up her hat. She placed it on her head and leapt back onto the stairs of the streetcar.

The shocked conductor could scarcely believe his eyes, but his astonishment quickly turned to anger.

"You shall sweat for this," the enraged conductor cried, pushing her against the wall.

In his next breath, he ordered the driver to "rise on the box and lash the horses" and do so without picking up any passengers. The car took off without Sarah, leaving Elizabeth alone with the conductor.

"Do not stop until we reach an officer or a station house," he cracked, with confidence.

They drove recklessly fast, sending riders sliding off their seats. The car bolted down Chatham, quickly passing Roosevelt, James, and Oliver Streets before the wide turn onto Bowery. On the corner of Walker, about a half mile from where they started, the conductor flagged down a policeman.

As the officer entered the bus, the conductor explained that his orders were to only allow colored persons onboard if none of the other passengers objected, and if they did, it was his job to show the black rider the door. Perhaps a handful of people remained on the bus when the officer asked if there were any objections. No one spoke out against Jennings in words or gestures. It seemed the only one who objected was the conductor.

Regardless, the officer wouldn't listen to anything Elizabeth had to say. He shoved her back toward the platform several times and then pushed her down the car stairs.

"I shall get redress for this," she yelled, holding her head up high.

"Do, if you can," laughed the policeman.

"What is your name?" she asked, pointing at the conductor.

"Moss, Edwin Moss," he replied, also giggling with delight.

The conductor wrote his name and "car No. 7" on a scrap of paper and threw it at Elizabeth, but she saw the number 6 painted on the side of the car. The officer then chased her off, "drove me away like a dog," she later recalled in her interview with the *American Woman's Journal*.

"Get out of the street," the policeman barked, "and don't be raising a mob or fight."

Beaten and torn, Elizabeth limped down Walker Street toward home. She passed a deserted coal and lumberyard, sawmill, and empty Panorama Hall. After a short distance, she realized a man was following her. Even on a Sunday afternoon, being alone on city streets with skip tracers abducting black women and children at will was risky and dangerous. Timidly the man approached and introduced himself.

"My name is Latour," he said in a thick German accent. "I witnessed the whole transaction in the street as I was passing. I live at 148 Pearl Street, where I am a bookseller."

Elizabeth trudged onward. Her spirits were lifted by the kind act of this stranger. She continued on, suffering yet determined that this day wouldn't be forgotten.

That afternoon, word of Elizabeth's brave stand and brutal assault quickly spread throughout the African American community. In a show of support, her church called a public meeting the next day to decide a course of action. Elizabeth was unable to attend the meeting herself because "I am quite sore and stiff from the treatment I received from those monsters in human form yesterday afternoon," she wrote from home.

In their annual reports to the state railroad commissioners, each rail line must catalog accidents under one of eight categories. "Fell or thrown from cars" was listed as a possible cause for death that must be reported by the railroad. In her absence, she provided a written statement about the attack that her father read. It served as a basis for newspaper accounts appearing in the *New-York Daily Tribune* and *Frederick Douglass' Paper*.

The meeting at the church was a lively expression of outrage, unity, and community empowerment. This was a time for action. By that, those attending meant legal action. Somehow the Third Avenue Railroad must be made to own up to the behavior of its employees and recognize "colored citizens [have] the equal right to accommodations of 'transit' in the cars," as the *Tribune* reported from the meeting in its July 19, 1854, issue. A committee organized by her father was formed to bring about a civil lawsuit.

All those present unanimously passed three resolutions. The first stated that the railroad's behavior was "intolerant" and called for the "reprehension of the respectable portion of the community." A second sought to sue the railroad and demanded a ruling on the legal status of African Americans using the transit system. The last resolution targeted media outlets such as the *Tribune* and *Douglass' Paper* to ensure that Elizabeth's case would be reported in the press.

Enthusiasm during the meeting ran high. It was time for free black New Yorkers to be recognized as equal citizens. Everyone in the audience knew that being able to go where you wanted when you wanted was the first step in reaching equality. But buried in those three resolutions was a dose of reality. The words "if possible . . . bring the whole affair to legal authorities" underlined the difficulties the group faced. Who would take on the cause of a black female looking for equality in a city bonded to the slave trade?

The proceeding closed on a spiritual hymn. The thoughts of everyone in the church were on the fallen schoolteacher at home humiliated and physically ailing. As they raised their voices in unity, it remained an open question if they would ever be heard beyond the church walls on Second Avenue and Sixth Street.

Chapter IX

The Trial

I told him . . . he was a good-for-nothing, impudent fellow who insults genteel people on their way to church.

—Elizabeth Jennings,
Letter to First Congregational Church Meeting

Elizabeth Jennings's name was now added to the long list of African American women physically beaten for attempting to use mass transit. Sojourner Truth, Harriet Tubman, and celebrated New England educator Susan Paul were among those attacked in a similar fashion.

Before Elizabeth was attacked, Truth nearly had her right shoulder blade broken by a Washington, D.C., conductor who slammed her against a door for entering a "whites only" streetcar. Tubman fought with a New Jersey railroad worker who lifted her from her seat and threw her into the baggage car like a sack of mail. Traveling to New York by steamboat, Paul was forced out of the ladies' cabin during a storm and caught consumption from spending the night on deck exposed to the elements.

Black men were victimized as well. Frederick Douglass was repeatedly pushed out of trains for sitting in white seats. The Reverend J.W.C. Pennington and David Ruggles grappled unsuccessfully with New York City conductors only to be abandoned miles from their destinations. Elizabeth's older brother Thomas Jr. was ordered out of the first-class seat he paid for and "threatened with violence from the conductor, baggage-master, brakeman, and one ruffian passenger," according to the June 19, 1841, edition of the *Colored American*.

Despite protests and editorials in the black press, these incidents fell on deaf ears. Conditions weren't improving. Manhattan's Board of Aldermen refused to consider any laws calling for equal access to transportation. Since emancipation in 1827, the New York State Legislature repeatedly voted against bills to provide free blacks full citizenship and end segregationist codes. Nationally, the Fugitive Slave Act put the freedom of every African American in the country at risk because it legalized kidnapping.

With few remedies available for a political solution, New York's free blacks were desperate for a human rights victory. Two men whose names are less familiar to historians but who played critical roles in this early fight for civil rights were Erastus Culver and Judge William Rockwell.

Culver arrived in Manhattan after a remarkable career as a congressman and abolitionist lawyer in upstate Union Village, New York, where he had listened to the Elder Arthur's sermons. As the slavery question boiled over, he moved his law practice to the metropolitan battlefront of Manhattan. A resident of Brooklyn, he immediately drew the scorn of his neighbors by attending freedom celebrations of West Indian blacks. He embraced their culture and condemned local churches for supporting slavery. Several years later, he was cast out as a member of the First Baptist Church of Williamsburg. Officially, the reason was visiting a widow after nine in the evening. More likely his abolitionist speeches angered the pro-slavery congregation, as reported in the *Brooklyn Eagle* on June 5, 1858.

Shortly after forming the Culver & Parker law firm, Culver faced a case that would test his abilities and would require extra support. In November 1852, slave owner Jonathan Lemmon was moving his family to Texas via the Port of New York. While they were waiting for their ship, Louis Napoleon, an African American furniture varnisher by trade, stunned Lemmon by petitioning for a writ of habeas corpus, claiming Lemmon's slaves were free. Napoleon surprised court workers with his detailed knowledge of the law.

To handle the legal paperwork and anticipated appeal process from the case, Culver took on a clerk, the son of a friend, who would eventually become a partner in the firm, Chester Arthur. By all accounts, the Lemmon trial was a sensation. The *New York Herald* noted, "The staircase and lobby of City Hall were crowded to excess" and drew "an immense crowd of colored persons." Culver's team argued that since residents of New York state couldn't own slaves, visitors weren't allowed to either. This meant any slaves who entered a free state would then become free.

When Judge Elijah Paine declared, "The eight colored persons mentioned in the writ, be discharged," the crowd erupted into cheers, "intoxicated with joy," according to the *New York Times*.

The Lemmon verdict stunned the South and put anti- and pro-slavery forces at violent odds across the country. In Boston, an angry abolitionist mob killed a US marshal while trying to free runaway slave Anthony Burns. They failed, but resistance and action were now replacing compromise as a means to bring about change.

The volatile national psyche must have weighed on Thomas Jennings's mind that spring. His youngest daughter was now a church organist. The pride he felt must have been tempered by his knowledge of the streets. Sixteen years earlier, his old friend Rev. Samuel Cornish warned the black community, "Brethren, attend to business by mail or go by foot."

In September 1852, Rev. J.W.C. Pennington, pastor of the Shiloh Presbyterian Church, echoed those thoughts in an open letter to the *New York Daily Times*. "I cannot avail myself of the use of any line of omnibuses," he stated, "or any of the multiplying lines of railways in the city." The Sixth, Eighth, and Harlem lines already resisted attempts to desegregate. Black activists such as Peter Bell were convinced the railways wanted to keep the races separate at a time when white ridership didn't really care. That meant a change in policy would bring little outcry from voters.

It's not clear if Elizabeth's confrontation was part of a larger plan to force a civil rights battle, but in any case, her lawsuit against the Third Avenue Railroad Company would be in the public eye for years to come.

After the church meeting on Monday, July 17, 1854, Elizabeth's father wrote an open letter from his newly formed Legal Rights Association, "To The Citizens Of Color, Male And Female, Of The City And State Of New York," to raise funds for her case. (His invitation to include women in the note shows how much his views on equal rights had evolved. Twenty years earlier, he signed a petition to ban females from anti-slavery activities.) In the end, her father had to foot the bill for her lawsuit, though its outcome would improve the lives of every black person in the state, and eventually the country.

In the note he states, "The assault, though a very aggravated case, is only secondary, in our view, to the rights of our people."

Thomas Jennings went on to point out that Elizabeth's case "will bring up the whole question of our [African American] right" to public transportation. He ends by stating, "Our opponents are rich and influential, we are the reverse, but our cause is just and we do not fear them."

In January 1854, the Third Avenue Railroad's secretary, Oscar F. Benjamin, reported that the year-old company was worth $1.7 million and that it took 3½ cents per passenger's nickel fee to break even, according to the *New York Daily Times*. In its annual report filed on November 15, 1855, the railroad stated that it carried nearly 5.9 million customers and made another $1,617.24 selling manure.

The failure of all the other transit civil rights lawsuits must have weighed heavily on Elizabeth Jennings's mind. Her brother's Boston experience from fourteen years before showed the need to be prepared for a legal fight. There was only one law firm that could stand against these odds in New York, if the family could afford it.

Not long after making his newspaper plea, Thomas L. Jennings retained Culver, Parker & Arthur to sue for his daughter's rights. As one of the most prestigious law firms in New York state, it was also one of the most expensive. To complicate matters, Culver was in the middle of his election controversy. If he became a judge, he wouldn't have time for her lawsuit.[7] To help offset legal costs, the firm's junior member, Chester Arthur, would argue his very first case on Jennings's behalf.

Then a surprising turn of events took place in the fall of 1854. Samuel E. Johnson was declared the winner over Culver, but Johnson chose not to serve. The only candidate remaining, Culver declared himself the winner with a little help. According to the *Sandy Hill Herald*, he "joined a Know Nothing Lodge, taking all the horrible oaths of secrecy without a qualm of conscience. By this adroit movement, he secured the office of Judge." They were called "Know Nothings" because members refused to comment on what happened during their secretive meetings. The party drew upon the fears in urban areas that immigrants would overrun the country. Irish Catholics and Germans were viewed as threats by the Know Nothings, who rallied to "America for Americans."

Nearly a decade earlier, New York state overhauled its courts from an agrarian traveling system of justices, or a circuit, to the courts we recognize today.[8] Instead of judges being appointed by the governor and visiting towns sporadically to wield justice in taverns or hotels, they would be elected by the people and serve in geographic districts with official courtrooms. The New York State Supreme Court became a statewide court of complete and original jurisdiction.

Arthur knew that to establish the right of African Americans to ride public transportation was as important to the Jennings family as holding the men who abused Elizabeth accountable. Tradition held that cases were tried in the locale where they happened. Since the incident took place on a Manhattan street and the Third Avenue Railway had its headquarters at No. 1 Ann Street, the assumption was that that was where the trial would take place. Arthur took away the home field advantage of the powerful railroad when he filed his court papers. Elizabeth Jennings's case against the Third Avenue Railroad would take place on February 22, 1855, in the Second District of the New York State Supreme Court in Brooklyn before Judge William Rockwell.

Brooklyn City Hall, now Borough Hall, was completed in 1848. The Second District of the New York State Supreme Court was also located there when *Jennings v. Third Avenue Railroad Company* was heard before Judge Rockwell.
LEAGUE OF LOYAL CITIZENS, 1895

Born on September 20, 1803, in Sharon, Connecticut, Rockwell came from a family of brilliant lawyers and jurists that could trace its roots back to the earliest settlers of America. Like Culver, his legal education was provided by an attorney with a strong abolitionist background (he clerked for Seth Staples, who worked on the *Amistad* case, which went before the US Supreme Court in 1841). With his law practice thriving, Rockwell turned toward politics. In 1845, he unsuccessfully ran for mayor, losing a three-way race to Thomas G. Talmage. Rockwell was part of the small but growing Native Party (the same Know Nothing Party that Culver had joined shortly before being elected as a judge).

Given their backgrounds, the circumstances of their elections, and their membership in the same secret society, it's likely Rockwell and Culver knew each other well. Culver's sudden party change raised some eyebrows. Some newspapers depicted Culver as an abolitionist kite flyer willing to tie any political party to his kite's tail to keep it aloft. Either way, it was an odd step for a man who was touted by some to fill the New York governor's seat as the upstart Republican Party candidate in 1858.

The morning of February 22, the weather was unusually pleasant after a frigid cold spell. Elizabeth and her father, perhaps with other family and community members in tow, likely made their way down to the Grand Street ferry for the fifteen-minute ride to Brooklyn. The one-penny trip across the East River was no picnic for blacks, who were routinely thrown out of cabins and seating.

Brooklyn was awash in American flags and parade bunting. At noon, cannons were fired from Brooklyn Heights and Fort Greene as the Veterans of 1812 marched down Joralemon Street in celebration of George Washington's birthday. No transcript or summary of the trial exists today. However, using newspaper articles, the events can be reconstructed.

The tall, slender Arthur was an imposing figure before Judge Rockwell as the court was called to session. It must have been a raucous atmosphere that day, with the building's rotunda filled with noisy parade-goers and fife & drum bands. In a retrospective article on Chester Arthur in 1880, the *New York Times* reported that "the courtroom was crowded almost to suffocation, and at one time serious trouble was threatened by those who believed that to seek justice for a black man was to do injustice to humanity."

Arthur would have called Elizabeth to the stand to establish the facts of the case for her claim of five hundred dollars. While documenting the incident for her congregation in the letter her father read aloud, Elizabeth took great care to mention her "respectability," and when the conductor tried to throw her off the horsecar, she noted, "I was born and raised here in New York." She then wondered aloud where he was born. Moss proudly stated "Ireland" before he attacked her.

A natural-born New Yorker with family roots back before the American Revolution, Elizabeth made a credible witness to a judge whose Native Party disdained immigrants, primarily the Irish.

In a surprise move, Moss and the driver pled no contest (admitted their guilt). There is no way of knowing if this admission caught the railroad's lawyers off guard or if they chose this path of defense. The Third Avenue Railroad claimed it wasn't liable for the actions of its employees. The judge seemed to agree with them, as the *New York Times* described years later.

"Pshaw," the *Times* reported Rockwell saying, "do you ask me to try a case against a corporation for the tort [wrongful action] of its agents?"

As Rockwell was about to pound his gavel upon the bench, Arthur must have thought of how far he had come. Just a few years before, he was in Cohoes with his chums trying to magnetize a table. Now he stood before a New York State Supreme Court judge with his first trial on the line. The following is based on information journalist Ben Perley Poore reported in the *Bay State Monthly*'s May 1884 edition.

"Your honor!" bellowed Arthur from across the courtroom.

Holding a book in his outstretched hand, he brought the court's attention to the Revised Statutes of the State of New York, Title XIII, Of The Law Of The Road, And Regulations Of Public Stages, Section 6, Owners of Certain Carriages Libel for Acts of Drivers. Silence hung over the courtroom as he read the following passage from a statute included in the Laws of 1824:

> *The owners of every carriage running or travelling upon any turnpike road or public highway, for the conveyance of passengers, shall be liable, jointly and severally, to the party injured, in all cases, for all injuries and damages done by any person in the employment of such owner or*

owners, as a driver, while driving such carriage, to any person, or to the property of any person; and that, whether the act occasioning such injury or damage be willful or negligent, or otherwise, in the same manner as such driver would be liable.

Arthur had them. More significantly, he had tweaked Rockwell with his acute understanding of the law. As Rockwell prepared to give the case to the jury to decide, the *New-York Daily Tribune* observed:

Judge Rockwell gave a very clear and able charge, instructing the Jury that the Company were liable for the acts of their agents, whether committed carelessly and negligently, or willfully and maliciously. That they were common carriers, and as such bound to carry all respectable persons; that colored persons, if sober, well behaved, and free from disease, had the same rights as others; and could neither be excluded by any rules of the Company, nor by force or violence; and in case of such expulsion or exclusion, the Company was liable.

It's highly unlikely every white passenger lived up to those standards, but the criteria were all-inclusive. Suddenly, the jury entered the courtroom. Their prompt decision silenced the crowd. Elizabeth and Chester sat next to one another quietly. As the foreman stood, father and daughter must have felt the weight of decades of broken promises on their shoulders.

The verdict was delivered: Elizabeth Jennings won the right to equal transportation.

As the courtroom erupted in cheers, Judge Rockwell would have restored order before moving forward. Because some members of the jury had "peculiar notions about colored people's rights," her $500 claim was reduced to a $225 settlement, to which the court added a 10 percent fee to cover legal costs. The railroad decided against an appeal. The railroad's comptroller, A.C. Flagg, must have grimaced. Just to recover the $250 payment, the Third Avenue would have to add at least another five thousand passengers. Segregation no longer made business sense, and the railroad ordered its workers to allow any paying customer to ride.

News of the triumph quickly spread. It caused such excitement that reportedly Horace Greeley, the publisher of the *New-York Daily Tribune*, wrote the headline "A Wholesome Verdict" and the article about the trial himself, ending with this bold statement:

> *Railroads, steamboats, omnibuses, and ferry-boats will be admonished from this, as to the rights of respectable colored people. It is high time the rights of this class of citizens were ascertained.*

Besides the *Tribune*, the *Brooklyn Eagle*, *Frederick Douglass' Paper*, and *National Anti-Slavery Standard* all covered Elizabeth's court case. Milwaukee's *Weekly Wisconsin*, reflecting on the "proper decision" of the Jennings verdict, reported: "the absurd and foolish prejudice against colored persons was rebuked, and their rights defended."

Her trial generated interest overseas in Europe and South America. For years afterward, in the African American community, February 22 was celebrated as "Elizabeth Jennings Day."

Chapter X

The Legal Rights Association

This action is brought . . . to test the question whether in this country, a colored man can or cannot ride in public conveyances.

—Frederick A. Tallmadge, to the Jury,
Pennington v. The Sixth Avenue Railway

Back in Manhattan, Thomas Jennings sensed a similar opportunity for marrying civil rights with community oversight. While Elizabeth's victory broke new civil rights ground and stunned Manhattan's railroads, the struggle wasn't over. The First, Second, and Fourth Avenue lines followed the example of the Third Avenue by opening their doors to all New Yorkers. The Legal Rights Association Jennings formed to fight for his daughter's cause also grew in stature when old friends J.W.C. Pennington and James McCune Smith joined the fray.

Pennington and McCune Smith saw transportation as the gateway to build African American freedoms. Streetcars provided the perfect opportunity for the races to meet on equal footing. It would take a concentrated effort by everyone in the community to be successful. Unexercised rights equate to no rights at all.

As far as the Legal Rights Association was concerned, Elizabeth's court victory was now settled law. As its president, Thomas Jennings was fully prepared to take each of the city's other public transit lines to court one by one if necessary. In May 1855, many other rights groups were holding conventions in Manhattan during "Anniversary Week." The LRA wanted all the black delegates to know they had the same right to ride as the next person. In what could be called an early press release, Pennington sent the following letter to newspapers around the country and also distributed it in the *Frederick Douglass' Paper*.

To the numerous colored ladies and gentleman who may visit this city during the coming anniversary week, let me say:

1. That all our public carrier-conveyances are now open to them upon equal terms.

2. No policeman will now, as formerly, assist in assaulting you.

3. If any driver or conductor molests you, by laying the weight of his finger upon your person have him arrested, or call upon Dr. Smith, 55 West Broadway, Mr. T.L. Jennings, 167 Church St, or myself, 29 Sixth-Av., and we will enter your complaint at the Mayor's Office.

4. You can take the conveyances at any of the Ferries, or stopping places. Ask no questions, but get in and have your five cents ready to pay. Don't let them frighten you with words; the law is right and so is the public sentiment.

J.W.C. Pennington

Using Elizabeth's success as a model, the LRA tracked incidents of transit discrimination, took surveys, fought onboard abuse, and raised funds. But lawsuits cost money, lots of it. Elizabeth did her part by appearing as a celebrity of sorts while playing the organ. Newspaper notices from the time promoted her performances as a way to draw an audience to social issues, merging entertainment with civil rights and fund-raising.

There were events such as the Literary Exhibition, "with subjects of the most thrilling interest, and unrivalled eloquence" sponsored by the Young Men's Literary Productive Society, which took place at the Sixth Street church on November 7, 1854, featuring "Miss Elizabeth Jennings at the Organ." For 12½ cents, the night included lectures on "The Elevation of the African Race" along with prayers and inspirational music such as "Old Hundred." Another event in 1856 was attended by three hundred patrons who danced and sang for the cause.

More often than not, though, the LRA was kept afloat with funds from its wealthier constituents, such as Thomas Downing, Jennings, and others. Years later in the *New York Age* newspaper, Elizabeth admitted that her father only collected seven dollars in donations to pay for her case. With so many causes that needed funding, the Gerrit Smiths and Tappans of the world were tapped out. The railroads and vested interests knew they could outspend the opposition.

To draw attention to the still-segregated railroad practices and document their civil rights violations, the LRA began holding public meetings in the summer of 1855. The first meeting was held at the Siloam Church on Prince Street in Brooklyn, Thursday, August 23, 1855. According to the *New York Daily Times*, inclement weather kept attendance down, but by nine p.m. about twenty people were there. Thomas Jennings, Dr. Pennington, and Reverend Amos Noë Freeman were among those representing the LRA.

The focus of the public's scorn was the Union Ferry Company and the Sixth Avenue Railroad's continued discrimination, as the *New-York Daily Tribune* observed.

> *The speakers spoke calmly, dispassionately of their wrongs and the great inconvenience they labored under . . . and also the insults they were liable to . . . The meeting was composed of the most intelligent colored citizens in our vicinity.*

Toward the end of the meeting that went on late into the night, Rev. Pennington made an impassioned plea for unity, as noted by the *Tribune*. "He hoped all colored citizens would join the Legal Rights Association, and they would all pull together. Thanks to Miss Jennings, who had obtained a verdict in Judge Rockwell's court."

The meeting ended with a unanimous resolution to continue fighting for their rights, and to enroll new members for an initiation fee of 25 cents plus a nickel a month in dues, according to the *New York Daily Times*. These meetings had the desired effect of arousing media interest while engaging the public. Laid bare, the abundance of abuses painted an unseemly portrait of the city's conveyances.

The biggest stumbling block to ending transit segregation in New York for good remained the Sixth Avenue line. It ran from Chambers Street up Sixth Avenue to Forty-Second Street to relieve traffic on Broadway.

Following Elizabeth's triumph, Rev. Pennington kept up the pressure on the railroads by urging his parishioners to ride city horsecars and omnibuses when and where they wanted. That spring, Sidney McFarlan, a black man from Church Street, was ejected from a Sixth Avenue streetcar and had the conductor and driver arrested. The judge dropped the assault charges, but later McFarlan won a civil lawsuit in Brooklyn against the company. Still, they wouldn't change their exclusionary policy.

Practicing what he preached, the forty-six-year-old Pennington boarded a Sixth Avenue bus on May 24, 1855. He was physically thrown off for sitting in car No. 22—meant for whites only. With help from the LRA, Pennington sued the railroad for one thousand dollars.

The Sixth Avenue Railroad knew it had a fight on its hands. Within days of the incident, company secretary T. Bailey Meyers fired off a letter to the mayor's office, reprinted in the *New York Daily Times*. In it, he accuses Pennington of demanding more than his race needs, and "even if he had the right [to ride freely], he would be wise to waive it" to spare those around him having to expose their prejudices and hurt his feelings. Meyers vowed never to give in: "We cannot admit, and shall not until a legal decision to that effect instructs us."

Still waiting for his trial in October 1855, Pennington sent a challenge to Sixth Avenue Railroad shareholders via the *Times*. He demanded reform, warning that petitions for legislation were circulating to create uniform passenger rights laws across all railways. The new rules would set fines for violators, stating, "If a colored man is worth $250 at the polls, he surely ought to be worth as much in the Sixth Avenue Railroad cars."

The laws weren't signed, and in many respects, Pennington's trial came too late. That summer, a yellow fever epidemic swept across Brooklyn. After a brief illness, William Rockwell collapsed in the arms of a fellow judge, vomiting blood. He died instantly on July 28, 1856, at age fifty-four.

If Elizabeth's trial caught the legal world by surprise, it was ready for Pennington's. The press seemed to be waiting for it too. Court cases were widely read in newspapers. The three-day affair was covered every day by the *New York Daily Times* under the headline "An Important and Interesting Trial—Can Colored People Ride in City Cars?" Pennington's litigation began on December 17, 1856, at the Superior Court building in lower Manhattan. Judge John Slosson, whose father once lost a piracy case to the infamous Aaron Burr, presided over the trial. Elected on the Whig Party ticket, he was viewed as a fair if not bland jurist.

Pennington was represented by one of the best legal minds available. Frederick A. Tallmadge knew his way around Manhattan politics and came from a distinguished family. He was a captain in the War of 1812, while his father ran a spy ring for George Washington during the Revolution. Tallmadge's opening statement was brief and to the point. This case wasn't brought to recover monetary damages, he said; it was about "whether or not in this country a colored man can or cannot ride these public conveyances."

Both sides produced witnesses to the events of that day. It's clear from comments made by the defense (Sixth Avenue) that the LRA was having an impact. Throughout the trial Pennington was accused of starting the lawsuit on behalf of the Association. The defense said the Association's goal was social change and had little to do with transportation.

Learning from Elizabeth's trial, the Sixth Avenue Railroad readily admitted it was a common carrier and must abide by those laws. By providing special cars for blacks and access to ride on all outside platforms, the railroad said it was obeying those rules. Allowing blacks to sit next to whites would cause the railroad to lose customers, it added. Pennington's team countered by conducting surveys showing that African Americans were underserved and that a majority of white riders raised no objection to black passengers.

Pennington's case went to the jury as the *Dred Scott* arguments were ending before the US Supreme Court. In his instructions to the jury, Judge Slosson made it clear that he saw the world differently than the late Judge Rockwell, as recorded by the *New York Daily Times* in its December 20, 1856, edition.

> *If it be true that this company is obliged by force of law, to admit colored people into their cars indiscriminately with the whites, I see no reason why a hotel-keeper is not equally bound to give any unoccupied room in his house to a colored man . . . The rights of citizens to be carried is not absolute. It is subject to such reasonable regulation as the carrier may prescribe.*

Slosson stated that the railroad was not obligated to allow any person to ride its cars who might seriously damage its business. Unlike in Elizabeth's case, the judge also said Pennington wasn't due damages for any injury he received trying to enter the bus after he was tossed out. Slosson told the jury that Pennington's actions negated his claim: "If he had peacefully left the car when ordered by the conductor to leave it, his legal right to this action would have been perfect as it is now [it] is after all his resistance [that is in] dispute."

Within hours, the jury returned its verdict. The Sixth Avenue Railroad prevailed, leaving the crushing grip of transit segregation on the city. It was a devastating blow to Thomas Jennings and his daughter. He was now sixty-five years old, and the years of abuse and struggle were taking a toll on him. He was no longer the nimble tailor of his youth. He stepped down as the Association's president, but the fight would continue with younger men.

One of the new leaders was Peter Porter, treasurer of the LRA and a school superintendent. He was badly beaten along with his wife and four other African American women while riding the Eighth Avenue line. Despite the Pennington setback, the Association kept the pressure on, forcing a lawsuit as complaints about the Porter incident grew. Eventually the Eighth Avenue railroad agreed to a settlement that included a change in its policy, allowing blacks to travel in all cars. The Ninth Avenue line followed suit. Even the dreaded Sixth Avenue line yielded to the inevitable. The New York State Legislature wouldn't prohibit segregated streetcars until 1873.

The railroads were beginning to understand what other New Yorkers already knew. Change was here. It came slowly at first, as did the light snow falling as fifteen hundred patrons drifted into the new Cooper Union lecture hall on February 27, 1860, to see Abraham Lincoln, shortly before he would become president. They came out of curiosity on a chilly Monday night to hear a lanky, disheveled Midwesterner address the issue of slavery.

Among others, on stage that night with Mr. Lincoln was Judge Erastus Culver. The last speaker of the evening, Culver was part of a group that showed the future president the streets of Manhattan. Those streets now belonged to all New Yorkers. The ordeals Elizabeth and the others faced to open the city's roadways would seem insignificant to the battles America was preparing to meet. Everything would be different from this moment on, but the struggle for equality by black New Yorkers continued.

Chapter XI

The Great School Wars

On the eve of commencing . . . what are my prospects? Shall I be a mechanic? White boys won't work with me. Drudgery and servitude are my prospective portion.

—Male Student,
History of the New-York African Free Schools

The Academy of Music on the north end of Fourteenth Street was the perfect place for the Female Normal School of New York City to hold its 1857 graduation commencement exercises. With its long Corinthian columns and rows of cathedral windows letting natural light flood in, the massive rectangular building symbolized power, openness, and the geometric symmetry of the great edifices built by ancient Greece—the very foundation of America's democratic culture.

It was located in a new part of town about two miles north of where the Jennings family lived. When Elizabeth was just a girl, real estate mogul Samuel B. Ruggles opened up the area for development when he purchased twenty-two acres of what was once the Gramercy Farm. To draw in the well-to-do, he named the area after his good buddy Washington Irving. Irving Place quickly became home to upper-middle-class bankers, lawyers, and importers, among others.

Elizabeth would get to see the toney conclave of Greek Revival and brick houses dotted around Gramercy Park on her way to the 1857 graduation ceremony. Although she had been teaching for several years, the Board of Education had recently required all teachers to complete a certification process. At the ceremony, she would receive her teaching certificate from the city's Board of Education for completing her normal school training. Prior to colleges developing teaching curriculums, normal schools coached promising high school and other students in the fine art of teaching. Elizabeth and her younger colleague Helen Appo were the first African American women to pass the rigorous training regimen required by the New York City Board. At the time, Elizabeth taught at Colored School No. 5 on Thomas Street in the City's Fifth Ward while Helen was a teacher in School No. 6 on Broadway near Thirty-Sixth Street in the Twentieth Ward.

The Board of Education operated three segregated normal schools: one for white males, another for white women, and a third for black females. This system was particularly hard on women because the female normal school classes were only scheduled from nine a.m. to one p.m. on Saturdays. On the other hand, classes for men were available Monday through Friday from four to seven p.m. Even though women were not permitted to teach after marrying, chores and attending to family members made weekend attendance problematic for many aspiring female teachers.

In the year she was certified, Elizabeth missed four of the twelve Saturday classes yet still managed to get a 1 (the highest grade) in each of her exam subjects: arithmetic, algebra, grammar, history, and astrometry. Only a handful of students among the two white normal schools accomplished this. Helen, her close friend, missed three lessons due to illness and performed nearly as well as Elizabeth during her exams.

Despite their accomplishments, the Board of Education's annual report for 1857 stated:

> *However, notwithstanding, this indication of improvement [Jennings/Appo], the general efficiency of this school is not satisfactorily. The encouragement derived from the visits, sympathies, and judicious counsels of School Officers seems very much to be needed by this School.*

But this wasn't a day to quibble. It was a day for celebration. According to various newspaper accounts, the event was oversold. The Board of Education reported that more than eight thousand people attended the ceremony, with "hundreds of others whom it was impossible to accommodate." The Academy of Music had seating for twenty-one hundred patrons. Pandemonium ruled the day. The reporter for the *Tribune* complained there were no accommodations made for the press. The five hundred student-teachers of the school assembled on the wide stage as families grappled for seats and floor real estate.

When the doors were finally shut for the program to begin, the heat began to build. The sound of flapping fans drowned out the speakers as a bucket of ice water was passed among the normal schoolmates to keep them steady on their feet. At seven p.m., the seventy or so graduands entered the hall in single file, singing as they made a procession to the back of the main stage in flowing white dresses. The ample lighting "showed off their rich and elegant costumes to the greatest advantage," according to the *New York Herald*. The *New York Daily Times* called the singing "very fair."

As the chanting of the Lord's Prayer began, it was apparent that something was missing. The two African American schoolteachers who earned the same degree as their white counterparts were pulled from the group and told by school administrators that they couldn't participate in the graduation ceremony.

Elizabeth's and Helen's names didn't appear with the other graduates listed in the newspapers the next day. No one knew they had earned their degrees. It was as if the two women never existed. Only three months after the *Dred Scott* decision by the US Supreme Court, they sat in a tiny room hidden from view listening to the chorus sing "Thoughts of Home," left to wonder if America could ever be home to them. Instead, they were handed diplomas alone after the festivities.

Such decisions are always political and supported by or issued from the top of an organization. While Elizabeth and Helen seethed in isolation, the president of the school board, Andrew H. Green, reported "in a rather long address the statistics of the Schools of the city and State." Boringly efficient, Green was known to favor the anti-slavery cause. However, he worked with quite possibly the worst New York City mayor in history, Fernando Wood. Within four years of this event, Wood asked the City Aldermen to secede with the Confederate States and form a blockade of Union ships. He committed many other indiscretions as well. Besides, Green already had his eye on becoming commissioner of the new Central Park project. Any negative publicity from white constituents complaining about amalgamation with blacks in schools could sink his chances.

Andrew Haswell Green was president of the New York City School Board in 1857. COURTESY MUSEUM OF THE CITY OF NEW YORK

A youthful experience may have also influenced Green's views on race and education. At age twenty-two, he went to Trinidad a decade after that country's slaves were freed to become a plantation manager. Through a combination of cultural myopia, racism, and naiveté, he couldn't understand why the freed Trinidadians didn't want to work hard on the ranchlands they were once enslaved on. He started a Sunday school hoping to instill Christian values and a work ethic in the populace.

None of the locals were interested. It would be one of the few failures Green would suffer during his working life, as he noted in his diary at the time. "The people are in fact too indolent to learn, though every means to be taken to interest and amuse them. They cannot attend steadily to instruction."

After the ceremony, Elizabeth was fuming and fired off a letter to old family friend William C. Nell, her brother's comrade in arms during their time in Boston. Nell became a journalist for the *Liberator*, *North Star*, and *Frederick Douglass' Paper*. He also authored a book, *Colored Patriots of the American Revolution,* and had become a powerful speaker against slavery.

News of the disgraceful treatment of Elizabeth and Helen also reached far beyond the local African American community. The week of August 4 through 6, 1857, the New York State Teachers Association held its twelfth annual convention in Binghamton, New York. The program began with the reading of various "pecuniary advantages" the association was able to pursue on behalf of male teachers.

When the moderator asked if any female teachers wished to speak, thirty-seven-year-old Susan B. Anthony stood up. Fully expecting a diatribe on voting rights, the audience hunkered down for a fight. Instead, Anthony read off a list of four resolutions related to the civil rights of African Americans.

The resolutions were included in Nell's August 21, 1857, article "Another Circumlocution Office."

> *1. Resolved, That the exclusion of colored children from our public schools, academies, colleges and universities, is the result of a wicked prejudice against color.*
>
> *2. Resolved, That a flagrant outrage was perpetrated against the teachers and pupils of the colored schools of New York City, in that no provision was made for their attendance at the free concerts given by Professor Thalberg to the public schools of that city.*
>
> *3. Resolved, That the recent expulsion of Miss Helen Appo and Miss Elizabeth Jennings, graduates from the Colored Normal School of*

New York City, from the public diploma presentation at the Academy of Music, was a gross insult to their scholarship and their womanhood.

4. *Resolved, That* all *proscription from educational advantages and honors, on account of color, is in perfect harmony with the infamous decision of Judge Taney,*[9] *that "black men have no rights which white men are bound to respect."*

Nell met Anthony in 1848 when he was working for the *North Star* in Rochester, New York (in 1851, it became the *Frederick Douglass' Paper*). Both Nell and Anthony became involved in the spiritualist movement as members of the "Rochester Circle," which also included at least one of the infamous Fox sisters and others. There was no help from beyond when the resolutions came up for a vote.

Despite a majority of the conventioneers stating they were in favor of the resolutions, after some deliberations and committee work, "the majority report was put to a vote, without consideration, and lost by a doubtful majority," reported Nell in the *Liberator*. No action was taken by the Teachers Association.

A week later, Nell wrote another scathing article that appeared in the August 28, 1857, edition of the *Liberator* under the headline "The Taney Hunt Against Colored Americans." In it, Nell returned to many of the same themes he reported from Binghamton. He notes the many "indignities heaped upon the unoffending colored man." Voter interference, job discrimination, and a politicalized court system all contributed to racism. "Ninety-nine percent of the outrages daily committed against freedom . . . in the name of American Democracy."

Nell chided the New York State Legislature for taking no action to protect the civil rights of African Americans.

The heavy head of proscription still presses upon them in the several departments of society, as at the Normal School for Girls, which had a grand exhibition a few days since at the Academy of Music, when the graduating class received their diplomas amid the cheers of an admiring crowd. Two young women, (Miss Helen Appo and Miss Elizabeth

> *Jennings), who passed a successful examination, were denied the privilege of appearing with their fellow-pupils, and sharing with them the pleasures and honors of the occasion, for no reason, except that God had given them a darker complexion than that of their sisters. On this account, they were compelled to receive their diplomas in private. This fact is disgraceful to the Board of Education, and a reproach to the city which does not with one voice protest against it.*

Inaction, lethargy—no matter what the cause, once again Elizabeth was confronted with bigotry. But instead of a loutish conductor, it was the learned men of the education board using statistics, rules, and subrogation to maintain the status quo. The hope of two women that education could foster equality was just another casualty in the ongoing war between white city leaders and the black community for control over their children's education.

Known as the Great School Wars, these battles—still erupting today—predate Elizabeth's tenure with their roots in the origins of the public-school system. While education was viewed as a right for the rich, as the nineteenth century progressed, the need for rudimentary schooling for workers was apparent. Affordable education on a mass scale was just what urban leaders wanted. It was not uncommon to have from five hundred to a thousand or more students in an open, factory-like room sitting in long rows with a monitor tending to each column. The Lancaster method (a development in education training popularized in London) ran schools with marching-band precision to optimize efficiency. Lessons relied on rote memorization and repetition—the perfect system to raise future troops for the British Empire's far-flung armies and navy. Such a system could only thrive in an environment of cooperation.

To accomplish that, the Lancaster method didn't resort to the harsh military discipline of the day. Instead, it relied on a series of incentives called tickets that rewarded and punished pupils accordingly. Tickets were valued at one-eighth of a cent. Rewards included books, tops, marbles, and mittens. The fine for talking was four tickets; disobedience, eight; truancy, twenty; and fighting, a whopping fifty tickets. Repeat offenders wore a six-pound log around their necks, were put in wooden shackles, or "occasionally, boys are put in a sack, or in a basket, suspended to the roof of the school," as John Franklin Reigart observed in his report on New York City education. This was early-nineteenth-century progressive thinking.

Charles C. Andrews was a divisive figure during his twenty years as head of the African Free Boy's School, popularly known as the Mulberry Street School. A white Englishman, he took pride in his five hundred students' accomplishments and showed empathy toward their frustration at not being hired for good jobs they were qualified to fill. Andrews gave a voice to their despair in 1830 when he wrote *History of the New-York African Free Schools*. At the same time, he often treated black parents as if they were children, reprimanding them "not to make promises they can't keep" and berating them in school plays for allowing his students to be late for class.

While the Manumission Society sought to exert control over the lifestyle choices of the black population, the Lancastrian system inadvertently helped develop the first wave of homegrown African American leadership. The Lancastrian system relied on student mentors to teach and put young students into positions of leadership in the classroom. As an eleven-year-old in 1824, James McCune Smith delivered a speech to General Lafayette and later became the first African American to receive a medical degree. Henry Highland Garnet was a preacher, abolitionist, and the first black person to address Congress. Patrick Reason, a well-known lithographer, took classes there, as did his brother Charles, a gifted mathematician and the first black professor at a white college.

All graduated from the African Free School under Andrews's watch. As the top students and monitors in their class, they taught their peers, negotiated with adults, and were looked to for guidance. They had high praise for their old principal. McCune Smith's comment about Andrews best summed up their feelings: "[He] held that his pupils had as much capacity to acquire knowledge as any other children . . . [his students] the object of his constant labors."

Andrews worked well with black community leaders to increase enrollment. Samuel Cornish functioned in an ombudsman role, providing the Society public feedback as he recruited more students for the African Free system, which had grown to five schools (the first burned down) in the early 1830s. Relations between the Society and community seemed to be improving, but it wouldn't end well for Andrews.

It all changed in early 1832 when a visitor came knocking on Andrews's classroom door. A young student named Sanders was asked to see who it was. Sanders returned to announce that a "colored gentleman" wished to speak with the principal. Andrews met the man and had a friendly conversation. After the visitor left, "Andrews caned the lad severely for having called a colored person a 'gentleman.'" With twenty years of leadership, no one had expected this behavior from Andrews.

The parents of the school's pupils were outraged. Caning, any physical punishment, was forbidden under Lancastrian rules. To have it occur over the use of the word "gentleman" raised more questions than it answered. The old scab was once again ripped off the wound of equality. African American businessmen and leaders called for Andrews's firing. Henry Sipkins, Thomas Jennings's good friend; William Hamilton, who delivered a rousing Jubilation Day speech four years prior; and Thomas Downing, the "Oyster King," all lobbied for Andrews's dismissal.

Although she was too young to recall much of the event, nearly sixty years later Elizabeth wrote to the *New York Age* about the incident, saying it marked a seminal moment when the black community unified behind a common cause. Speaking as one voice, the parents threatened to pull all their children from the Society's schools if Andrews wasn't replaced by an African American educator. In the spring of 1832, Andrews was let go and one of his students, John Peterson, took over. Peterson's teaching staff was nearly all black, and the following year, enrollment jumped to nearly 1,450 students.

The first battle of the Great School Wars was won with community resolve and cohesion. But it was only the opening sortie in a protracted tug-of-war. The same way the growth rings of a tree tell the story of its environment, so too did Elizabeth's career reveal the scars of every racial conflict.

By the time Elizabeth was old enough to teach, the City's Common Council had long ago ended its funding support for the African Free School buildings. The Manumission Society bequeathed its administrative role to the Public School Society (a charitable organization), which changed the school's name from African Free to the Colored Public Schools. Once again, black education was allowed to flounder with minimal resources and inferior facilities. There wasn't one high school in the city that African American students could attend.

In 1848, Elizabeth student-taught under Fanny Tompkins in the Girls Department at Colored Public School No. 2. The following year, she went with a new organization, the New York Society for the Promotion of Education among Colored Children. The names of those running the new society were familiar to Elizabeth. They were associates of her father: McCune Smith, Sam Cornish, and John Peterson. Elizabeth settled in at the Promotion's School on Thomas Street, working under the tutelage of Charles Reason. In 1850, Elizabeth had a homecoming of sorts, returning to the basement classroom at St. Philip's Church where her family went to school years before. Because of a shortage of teachers, she was acting principal for a while, perhaps the first black woman ever to do so. Her annual salary of $225 would stay the same for nearly a decade—roughly half of what white teachers were paid.

In April 1851, the *North Star* published a report on the state of black education in New York City that had been presented at the Convention of Citizens of Color held in Albany, New York. The report detailed the number of black students enrolled in the Public School Society, Society for Promotion of Education, Ward Schools, the Colored Orphans Asylum, and Alms House classes. With a total of just 3,339 pupils, the report concluded that "the city of New York has provided instruction and school accommodations for about one-eighth of the whole colored population."

Elizabeth returned to the Thomas Street School for the following two years to work with Charles Reason again. She would report to him at numerous times throughout her career. Meanwhile, enrollment in the Promotion's Schools was steadily increasing, with attendance reaching almost one thousand students. Despite this progress, the Common Council decided to consolidate all the city's private and parochial schools under the auspices of an independent Board of Education. With no funding from the city, all the black instructional entities ceased operation and ceded their charters to the new Board of Education.

Shortly after taking over, the Board announced in its annual manual that "no teacher shall be hereafter employed in any of the Ward Schools that has not received a certificate of qualifications." To earn that diploma required a two-year or four-semester commitment. The teachers took five to seven classes, with the hardest courses noted as A's and the easiest as E's. Exams were held every spring and winter. The minimum age to enter the normal school was fourteen for males and sixteen for females.

The abuse showed the commencement program's first two black graduates didn't deter them. They both came from successful, hard-working families. Elizabeth had already stood up for her civil rights, and perhaps because of that, had to endure this indignity. Ten years older than Helen, she must have realized that she was now the mentor her sisters and the members of her mother's old literary society were once to her. Soon Frederick Douglass would note in his paper that Elizabeth was "the most learned of our female teachers in the city of New York."

She was now a veteran of the school wars that would rage on throughout the rest of her life. Helen too joined the battle. As Helen Appo Cook, she became president of the Colored Women's League in Washington, D.C., and helped create its successor, the National Association of Colored Women. Her decedents were longtime trustees of Howard University.

At the turn of the century, Helen wrote a pointed letter to Susan B. Anthony about race, perhaps unaware of their kindred connection from forty years earlier. Someone once said that war turns vanities into virtues. It remained to be seen in a society dominated by male pride if the influence of female educators could win the day and bring equality for all.

Chapter XII

The Civil War Comes to New York

Let the verdict of death which has been brought in against slavery be affirmed and executed by the people. Let the gigantic monster perish . . . And leave no traces where it stood.

—Henry Highland Garnet,
Let the Monster Perish

At this point, Chester Arthur had gained fame. He was now a man about town. His victory against the Third Avenue Railroad, and as the attorney of record on the Lemmon appeal, made him a hero to Manhattan's black community.

Arthur's social life picked up as well. A friend of a roommate at the Bancroft House vacationing in Manhattan invited him to a party. At this party Arthur met Ellen ("Nell") and fell in love. Nell was a classic Southern belle. An only child, she was born into an aristocratic Old Dominion family in Virginia. Her mother's Hansbrough roots went back to twelfth-century England. Nell had style and grace and was a beauty to boot. She sang and mingled with Washington, D.C.'s, cognoscenti. Her father, Navy captain William Lewis Herndon, was a veteran of the Mexican War and famous for exploring the Amazon River.

In short, the Herndons were everything the Arthur Clan wasn't. Chester was hooked deeper than any pike or freshwater bass he once reeled in from the upstate streams of his youth. The Herndons summered in Saratoga Springs, New York, not far from where he dropped out of law school three years before for lack of funds. The Herndons owned a slave and rubbed elbows with the old money in Newport, Rhode Island. They were way above his pay scale, but Chester wouldn't be deterred.

Two years later, tragedy struck the Herndon family and altered the course of Chester's life. To support Nell in the manner she was accustomed to, Arthur had to accumulate wealth quickly. He headed west to Kansas with his law partner Henry Gardiner for the "land grab." During this period, Captain Herndon was piloting the SS *Central America*, a massive 750-ton, three-mast, 272-feet-long sidewheel steamship. It was operated by the U.S. Mail Steamship Company and therefore required a naval officer at the helm.

During its service, the ship carried a third of the gold mined in California during the rush, worth about $150 million at the time. This was the nineteenth run Herndon would make from Panama to New York City. Nearly five hundred passengers boarded for the journey from Havana, Cuba, to the United States. Along with them were an estimated twenty-one tons of gold and thirty-eight thousand pieces of mail.

The trip began on a sultry day on September 8, 1857. The rough seas didn't faze the experienced captain, who went about his business with steely resolve. By the next day, conditions worsened. Waves washed over the gunwales, flooding the lower decks. The crew and passengers tried to bail the water out using bucket brigades. In the early morning, Herndon had distress flags hoisted and flare guns fired. The brig *Marine* answered their call. By then, three of the *Central America*'s lifeboats (built to hold fifty people) were smashed to bits by the fierce waves. Herndon ordered women and children first, with the hope that the boats could shuttle the remaining crew to the *Marine*, but the fifty-knot winds and high waves it drove were too strong.

At eight p.m. on September 12, Herndon went down with his ship and 425 others 160 miles off the coast of Cape Hatteras, North Carolina. With more than fifty million dollars in expected gold missing, New York banks and businesses began defaulting on loans, triggering the "Panic of 1857." Overwhelmed with grief and pride in their fallen comrade, the US Naval Academy in Annapolis, Maryland, erected a gray granite obelisk much like the one standing some 250 miles north in Cypress Hills at the Jennings plot. It bears this epitaph under the commodore's plaque: Forgetful of self, in his death he added a new glory to the annals of the sea. (Herndon likely would be proud that his monument is part of the annual "plebes-no-more" ceremony to mark the end of the freshman year. Plebes work as a team to climb the greased thirty-three-foot obelisk to replace a sailor cap on its top.)

Nineteenth-century life was tough on widows and children no matter the class of people. Suffering from fatigue and shortness of breath, Elizabeth Jennings's father became bedridden. He was afflicted with anemic hepatitis, and there was little nineteenth-century medicine could do. Rest and potions of milk thistle were about the only treatments available. His condition worsened. On Friday, February 11, 1859, he died at the age of sixty-eight—the gold-framed "Letters of Patent" hanging on the wall above him.

In death, Jennings served his community one last time. To honor his fallen brother, Frederick Douglass used the occasion to praise Jennings in the *Anglo-African* newspaper.

> *Mr. Jennings was a native of New York, and in his early youth was one of the bold men of color who, in this slave State, paraded the streets of the metropolis with a banner inscribed with the figure of a black man, and the words, "AM I NOT A MAN AND A BROTHER?"*

Douglass went on the say, "This is a noble picture of a noble man . . . He was not an exception, but a representative of his class, whose noble sacrifices, and unheralded labors are too little known to the public." Jennings led "an active, earnest and blameless life." Douglass also stated that Jennings was "not gifted with extraordinary talents." However, his point was not to belittle Jennings, but to rebuke white abolitionist Gerrit Smith for his comments in another publication, "The mass of blacks are ignorant and thriftless." Douglass asked Smith to retract his statement to honor Jennings's memory. Increasingly, white abolitionists had to come to terms with treating freed blacks as political and social equals.

Jennings was laid to rest at a noontime service on February 14, 1859. He purchased a large family plot at the recently opened Cypress Hills Cemetery in Brooklyn. Years before, burials were banned on Manhattan Island and many graves were relocated outside the city limits. His name was added to a black granite obelisk bearing those of family members who passed before him. (The family name on the obelisk is spelled "Jinnings," although its members are engraved as "Jennings.") The inscription was simple, yet summed up the total of his life's work: Thomas L. Jennings, Defender of Human Rights.

Only a decade before, women were granted the right to own property and gain inheritances in New York state. This was done more to protect the father's fortune from a scheming husband than to recognize females as equals. After her father's death, Elizabeth and her mother moved to 541 Broome Street and opened the Empire State Hotel and Union House.

After her father's ship went down, Ellen asked Chester to return from Kansas to New York to settle her family's affairs. A violent incident made the two rube lawyers realize the Wild West wasn't for them. They traded cowboy boots for cobblestones back in New York.

Shortly before the Civil War started, Sarah Jennings Smyth relocated to San Francisco. She and her husband, Samuel, took over the operation of an upscale resort on Broadway called the Lodge House. Located in the Barbary Coast district near the waterfront, it catered to the growing population of black entertainment workers in the area. For several years, Lodge House advertisements ran under Samuel's name in the weekly *Pacific Appeal*, one of the country's largest black newspapers. Witnessing the transit discrimination African Americans faced in California, Sarah sent newspaper clippings from Elizabeth's trial to the paper's editors. The articles were reprinted in 1863 as an inspirational "how to" example for community groups.

(Elizabeth's other sister, Matilda, may have settled in California as well. Advertisements for a dressmaking and sewing shop on Mission Street owned by a Mrs. Matilda Thompson also appeared in the *Appeal* during this time frame. No mention of a husband suggests she may have been widowed or divorced. Other family news was shared and printed by the newspaper too.)

Prior to the Civil War, Elizabeth Jennings met a twenty-six-year-old man from St. Croix. According to census records, a Charles Graham was an apprentice tailor on Hill Street in Christiansted. During the 1850s, Graham had made his way to New York. After a mourning period for her father, Elizabeth and Charles were married on June 18, 1860. Despite Board of Education bylaws that stated "if a woman teacher should marry, charges might be preferred against her by reason of such marriage," Elizabeth Jennings Graham demanded that she should be allowed to stay on in her position.

The view of the education board's position is made even clearer in its report on female education. According to records in its archives, *to educate a woman above her station is a disadvantage to her, and to those with whom she may be connected by family ties. The danger of disturbing the equilibrium of the marriage relation may be dwelt upon especially in this connection.*

As for a woman's lot in life, her elevation "is dependent upon the success in business . . . of her father, her brother, or husband. She herself, if over-educated, only rendered the more unhappy."

Principal Charles Reason rewarded her gumption with a raise and promotion to his second-in-command.

Marriage was certainly on Chester's mind when he ran the gauntlet of Southern propriety, meeting all the Herndons, near-Herndons, Hansbroughs, and then some down in Virginia. Arthur may not have had money, but he played the part well. Impeccably dressed, with a quick wit and genteel manner, he won over the extended Herndon family. Not to mention that he somehow managed to master the byzantine bookkeeping and legal issues the family faced. Having also observed the proper mourning period, Chester and Ellen were married on Tuesday, October 25, 1859, in Manhattan's Calvary Episcopal Church by the Reverend Dr. Pyre from Washington, D.C. They settled in at a home on Twenty-First Street owned by the Herndons. The next time Arthur would see his wife's relatives, the setting wouldn't be quite so cordial.

Within two years of marrying, the Grahams had a son, Thomas L., named after Elizabeth's late father. Some historians believe the boy was adopted. Records show that Elizabeth never took any time off from teaching to bear a child (pregnant women weren't allowed to work either). In addition, there was no birth certificate filed for him. There is a chance the couple were following an ancient African tradition by taking in an orphaned or abandoned child from the community and raising him as their own.

The Arthurs also had an infant son about the same age. They named him William to honor both families' patriarchs.

Ellen Lewis Herndon in 1859. Nell had class, style, and family bloodlines. She was also a protégée of an elderly Dolly Madison, who loved her singing voice. LIBRARY OF CONGRESS

Joy was again mixed with sorrow for Elizabeth. Her older brother Thomas Jr. was arrested in November 1860 for "giving expression to sentiments calculated to produce discontent and insubordination amongst slaves," as reported by the *Daily True Delta.* The charge brought by the chief of police carried a potential death sentence. Eventually the case against him was dropped.

The following May, the same police chief charged Thomas Jr. and his second wife, Angelina Augusta, with improperly attending a church fair where they ate ice cream and cake in the presence of whites. According to the *New Orleans Daily Picayune*, several white witnesses came forward to vouch for the Jenningses, stating, "There was nothing intruding or disrespectful in their conduct." Although Louisiana was now part of the Confederate States, the New Orleans district attorney saw no wrongdoing and again sought no trial. Instead, he wondered why the white fair organizers would improperly invite a black couple.

Despite building a successful career and serving communities in Boston and New Orleans, Dr. Jennings suffered from the strain and stress of constant harassment from authorities. Once listed in the *Daily Picayune* as one of the top one hundred gentlemen of New Orleans, Thomas L. Jennings Jr. died at age forty-nine on January 29, 1862. The *Daily Picayune* reported his death, as it had his many stands against oppression.

Shortly before noon on Friday, February 21, 1862, the mournful din of military drums was heard echoing inside the courtyard of the Halls of Justice, known as the Tombs. A detachment of armed marines marched past the wooden gallows and took up their places guarding exits into the prison. Bayonets fixed for battle, they stood ready to defend the proceedings against an angry mob milling about the Five Points, where the Tombs was located.

The prison earned this nickname because its design was supposed to resemble an ancient temple. Upon visiting it, a horrified Charles Dickens called the structure a "dismal-fronted pile of bastard Egyptian." In almost twenty-five years of service, it earned a reputation as the worst jail in the country. Housing more than three hundred of Manhattan's toughest criminals, its grounds witnessed many executions. However, none was more shocking than one about to take place that afternoon.

The trial of Captain Nathaniel Gordon divided the city's residents as no other had. Caught at sea aboard the *Erie*, Gordon traded 150 hogsheads[10] of whiskey for 897 Congolese lives. Despite slave trafficking carrying a sentence of death, no one ever convicted of slave trading received more than a small fine or short (often-pardoned) jail term. Gordon expected no less, especially in a city where its mayor, Fernando Wood, boldly recommended to the common council that Manhattan follow South Carolina's lead and secede from the United States. The rubber stamp board approved Wood's plan, heeding his earlier words, "The profits, luxuries, the necessities—nay, the physical existence of [the city] depend upon the continuance of slave labor and prosperity of the slave master."

Others helped the legal system look the other way. James J. Roosevelt I was a known slavery sympathizer. The US District Attorney for New York, he often let accused slave traders plead to lesser or dismissed charges. This courtesy was extended to Gordon, who promptly turned it down. Already able to walk around town and dine at fine restaurants by bribing guards, according to US Marshal Robert Murray, Gordon said he was "not as a felon, but as a gentleman temporarily out of his latitude."

Gordon badly overplayed his hand. The jury was dismissed during his first trial. More significantly, in April 1861, the newly formed Confederate States fired upon Fort Sumter. The Civil War had arrived, causing many to rethink their position on Gordon and slavery. The differing views of New Yorkers were reflected in their newspapers.

On the pro-slavery side were the *New York Herald* and *New York Daily News* (owned by Mayor Wood's brother). They blamed free blacks for the city's troubles and roused the working class by predicting that ex-slaves would flood Manhattan's job market, displacing whites. To them, Gordon was a businessman providing economic opportunity for all. The *New York Times* and *New York Tribune* led the way for anti-slavery and pro-Union sentiment.

The Lincoln administration aggressively pursued the captain. A new attorney replaced Roosevelt, and Gordon was convicted on November 9, 1861. Particular care was taken to ensure that Gordon was treated as humanely as possible. A gallows known as the "Upright Jerker" was used because it instantly broke a man's neck without leaving him to dangle at rope's end. The mob was kept outside the prison, where liquor and trinkets were sold as if it were a sporting event. P.T. Barnum anxiously waited to bribe officials for a death mask and shreds of clothing to exhibit at his bizarre museum down the road.

Weakened by a suicide attempt, Gordon was escorted by guards to the noose. As the black hood was pulled over his face, Murray reported that Gordon said, "Make the knot run easy, and fix it on the right." At twelve thirty, the commander waved his saber and the cord was cut, snapping Gordon's body four feet into the air. With his life ended two hundred fifty years of a slave trading economy in New York City.

Gordon's execution marked the beginning of an uneasy time in Manhattan. With the economy in shambles, workers displaced, and the war going poorly, the city was ready to erupt.

The war was now part of everyone's lives. Early hopes for a negotiated end to the fighting vanished with the rout of Union troops at Bull Run. Once again, New York City began to remake itself. Having voted to secede and prevent Union troops from crossing its borders in 1861, the city volunteered sixty-six regiments to aid the war effort. New York became the center for the wheels of war, funneling uniforms, weapons, food, and supplies through its port.

Without a steady hand in control, such ventures were ripe for corruption and fraud. Arthur, now a well-known lawyer in Republican political circles, was appointed quartermaster general for New York state by Governor Edwin Morgan. Arthur now faced a predicament many Americans did during the Civil War. His Virginian wife's family sided with the South. Several of the Herndons' and Nell's other relatives served in the Confederate Army, as did Chester's sister Malvina's husband, Henry.

At parties, Arthur laughingly called Nell "my little Confederate" or his "rebel wife." But it was no joking matter when Nell's cousin ended up in a Union prison camp on an island near New Rochelle, New York. Nell pressured Arthur to pull some strings to allow her to visit her cousin on David's Island. Her slave-owning family's views dampened Arthur's abolitionism as he drifted away from his father's unyielding values. Nell showed him the elegance and finery that came with power and money.

No longer quartermaster for the state under the new Democratic administration, Arthur returned to private law practice in the lucrative field of war reparations. Arthur never enjoyed trial work. His law firm didn't have a bevy of clients, but the ones he had he chose well. When Lewis Tappan sold his Mercantile Agency to his brother-in-law Robert Graham

Dunn in 1859, it became R.G. Dunn & Company. (In 1939, the firm merged and became Dunn and Bradstreet.) Perhaps trading on his abolitionist background, Arthur retained the firm as one of his lifetime clients. He also legally protected the family jewels of Charles Lewis Tiffany.

The war changed the lives of others as well. Elizabeth continued to raise a family at her mother's boardinghouse and teach at Colored School No. 5 on Franklin Street. By 1863, many New Yorkers felt devalued by the war. Always a barometer of the city's temperament, the waterfront exploded into violence that spring. Irish workers attacked black longshoremen over jobs they felt belonged to them. For two hundred fifty years, fists ruled the city's piers as one ethnic group battled another for turf and supremacy. However, this time it was different. The Irish mob sought to destroy any blacks working or living in the area regardless of their connection to the docks.

The flames of racial hatred fanned by newspapers since Gordon's trial continued to push for violence. Nearly two-thirds of the city's newspapers were supporters of the South called Copperheads. These papers blasted the Emancipation Proclamation, which freed all the slaves held in the Confederacy, as the first step toward blending the races. Cartoons and pamphlets depicted black men and white women dancing romantically at "miscegenation balls."

Ironically, the group most associated with persecuting African Americans was also among their most supportive. Frederick Douglass learned the power of oration in the 1840s listening to Irish nationalist Daniel O'Connell. O'Connell invited Douglass to Ireland, where he helped Douglass raise money for his freedom.

Hoping to control the mercurial Douglass overseas, Maria Weston Chapman of the Boston Antislavery Society wrote a letter to his Irish publisher, Richard Webb, asking him to watch Douglass. Being a good Irishman, Webb handed the letter to Douglass as soon as he arrived. In Ireland, Douglass felt empowered as never before. Overflow crowds of working-class Dubliners came to hear him speak and purchased his book *Narrative* in record numbers. He wrote that he went from being "shut out from the cabins of steamboats . . . to sharing cabs with white people."

Yet the goodwill and compassion from Ireland didn't cross the Atlantic with its immigrants. Some historians point to natural friction between two groups at the bottom of the social ladder as the cause for decades of hostilities, but the facts don't support this. Statistics from 1855 show that in each job category the African American presence in New York City was minor compared to the Irish.

In the summer of 1863, the city truly erupted. It all started on Saturday, July 11, with the announcement that the long-awaited draft lottery would begin. The drawings were scheduled by district and took place at the US Marshal's office on Third Avenue and Forty-Seventh Street. Conscription became necessary to provide more troops as the war dragged on.

The Enrollment Act of 1863 made all men between the ages of twenty and thirty-five eligible for duty. Those selected randomly were expected to serve, with two exceptions: if the drafted man found a substitute to take his place, or he paid three hundred dollars for an exemption. The working poor felt betrayed by the city's Copperhead Democrats, who said this would never happen, and victimized by abolitionist Republicans, who passed the law. In *Diary of a Union Lady*, Maria Lydig Daly recalled white laborers roaming the streets shouting, "[We] are sold for $300 whilst they pay $1,000 for Negroes."

Conditions were ripe for trouble. With most of New York's garrison called away to face General Lee's advancing army in Pennsylvania, the city was defenseless. At the US Marshal's headquarters, names were placed in a large, hand-cranked drum. William Jones, living on Forty-Sixth Street, was the first of twelve hundred names selected that day. The proceedings ended at four o'clock with the crowd mostly in good spirits talking about the Union victory at Gettysburg the week before. A Sunday off to ponder and drink changed the public mood considerably.

Draft selection for the Ninth District was scheduled to start again at eleven o'clock on Monday, July 13. Hours earlier it became apparent that few people were showing up for work. Eighth and Ninth Avenues teemed with disgruntled workers making their way uptown. As was the custom, the crowd stopped at each shop and business along the way urging its workforce to join them. Those who didn't assemble to join the protest were beaten and their businesses looted.

As the mob reached Third Avenue, telegraph lines were cut and tracks from the Second, Third, and Fourth Avenue railroads uprooted. Shortly after the lottery began, the Black Joke Engine Company No. 33 showed up in full parade uniforms. (*Black Joke* [or *Joak*] was a five-gun sloop that captured several British ships during the War of 1812. It was named after a rather bawdy Irish street song popular since the 1730s.) They demanded a firefighter's exemption from service as gunshots rang out. Suddenly the firemen stormed the office smashing the lottery equipment and setting the building ablaze.

The rioters spread out across the city. At first content to destroy draft machinery and locations, by Monday afternoon the crowd began burning the homes of policemen. Anyone suspected of helping government workers was beaten senseless. To make matters worse, street corner politicians stood on soapboxes whipping the crowd into a frenzy. According to the *New York Tribune* on July 13, 1863, "An attack was made upon colored men and boys in every part of the city . . . crowds of 100 to 500 persons hunted them like bloodhounds. Several inoffensive colored men were dragged off city cars [streetcars] and badly beaten." Less than a mile from Elizabeth's home, a nine-year-old African American boy at the corner of Broadway and Chambers Street was attacked by a gang. While he was battered with sticks and rocks, the *Tribune* reported, the boy "jumped on a two-horse wagon that was passing by" and was believed to have escaped.

A midtown mob descended upon the Colored Orphans Asylum on Fifth Avenue. Built in 1836 by Quaker women, it housed more than 230 homeless children in a large, four-story complex. To appease the mob, the orphanage caretakers came out holding a white flag of truce. To their surprise, many of the rioters were women and young boys. The crowd wouldn't listen. With no time to lose, the orphans were hurried out the back through a garden where young Irish firefighter Paddy M'Caffrey along with several coachmen drove the children to safety. A frightened girl found hiding under her bed by the rioters was murdered instantly. Her lifeless body was thrown into the street.

In less than two hours, the building was ransacked and burned to the ground. As the terrified children made their way into the Thirty-Fifth Precinct police station, a *New York Times* reporter observed,

The Colored Orphans Asylum was located on Fifth Avenue and Forty-Second Street and and had the capacity to house four hundred children. COURTESY NEW YORK PUBLIC LIBRARY

> *dozens of men, or rather fiends, among the crowd who gathered around the poor children and cried out, "Murder the d -- d monkeys," "Wring the necks of the d -- d Lincolnites."*

The mob was now in control of the city. Gangs freely prowled Thompson, Leonard, and Nassau Streets chasing African American families from their homes and torching entire neighborhoods. A heavy, soot-laden, black smoke clung to the city like a shroud, making it hard to breathe. If not for a sudden downburst of heavy rain that night, flames would have engulfed lower Manhattan. Many of these stories were memorialized by the Committee of Merchants for the Relief of Colored People Suffering from the Late Riots. The following testimony was taken from a Mrs. Statts:

> *As they surrounded us, my son exclaimed, "Save my mother, gentlemen, if you kill me." "Well, we will kill you," they answered; and*

> *with that two ruffians seized him, each taking hold of an arm, while a third, armed with a crowbar, calling upon them to stand and hold his arms apart, deliberately struck him a heavy blow over the head, felling him . . . on Broome Street I encountered another mob, who, before I could escape commenced stoning me. They beat me severely.*

They tore off her dress, stoning her until she was unconscious.

Not far away, Elizabeth and her family tried to wait out the madness. She had other concerns as well. Her son, just learning to walk and talk, was having difficulty breathing. The gunfire, screaming crowds, and agony in the streets upset the boy. He developed a fever and shook in spasms at times. Dr. James B. Wyckoff, who lived a few doors away, diagnosed Thomas with "convulsions." While a serious aliment, it was thought to be caused most often by teething or a colicky stomach. Treatments included warm baths or a drop of tincture (a mixture of herbs and alcohol) in a half glass of water.

Rather than calm the residents from the riots, the *Metropolitan Record* suggested that further resistance was possible: "There are, we should think, arms enough in this city to supply at least twenty thousand men." The rioting continued. On the street near Pfaff's Beer Hall, two hundred policemen defeated a mob of five thousand, killing some of its organizers. Four blocks from Elizabeth's home, seven hundred rioters attacked black residents on Baxter Street. Mary Williams, a black prostitute, leapt through a glass window at No. 74 Roosevelt Street as a gang pursued her. According to Iver Bernstein, Alfred G. Jones, director of the Sixth Avenue Railroad, wrote in his diary that he was seized from his office and dragged before the mob. He faced the same loutish behavior his company asked African Americans to endure just a few years before.

By Thursday, July 16, little Thomas's condition seemed to deteriorate along with the city's. A weeklong illness took its toll. He fell unconscious, his face turned ashen, and his tiny hands clenched into fists as his body twitched and lips turned blue. Thomas's breathing grew fainter and fainter until, finally, Dr. Wyckoff pronounced the boy was dead.

Two miles uptown, tragedy struck another family at 123 Lexington Avenue. Just one week before, the Arthurs lost their only son to the same disease. Chester wrote to his brother, "We have lost our darling boy." He felt guilty that he had overheated the boy's brain with demanding educational tasks for a two-year-old. The boy's death added to Chester's growing yoke of guilt.

For the rest of his life, he blamed himself for William's death, claiming that he pushed the lad too hard. Devastated by William's loss, the Arthurs left town before the riots began to bury their son at the Rural Cemetery in Albany, New York.

Elizabeth was no less determined to treat her son with the respect he deserved. Despite the dangers of ongoing rioting, she planned a noon funeral on Monday, July 20, at the historic St. John's Chapel, a part of Trinity Church. This was done because the police were still using her church, St. Philip's, as a command post and barracks during the riots. The Reverend Alvah Wiswall, who worked with the parish poor, performed the service.

It was equally difficult to find an undertaker willing to risk such a dangerous assignment. There were at least two morticians who catered to the black community: Andrew Duncan, himself African American, and John Winterbottom. Both sustained serious injuries during the rioting. The two of them cobbled together enough resources to handle the child's funeral.

The hearse was usually a black carriage with a glass-encased bed. As was the custom for infants, Thomas was most likely buried in a white casket in the center of the family plot next to his grandfather for protection.

The smoldering world Elizabeth looked upon, as the funeral carriage made its way down Varick Street toward Brooklyn, was far different from the one she saw only a week before. Because of the riots, African Americans were temporarily suspended from riding streetcars and trains for their own safety. City rail systems gradually reinstated their policies to allow blacks to ride at will. The last known discrimination case pitted Ellen Anderson against the Eighth Avenue Railroad in 1864. Widow of a Civil War hero, she easily won her case, according to the *New York Times*. Restored, that right was never questioned again in New York City.

Street corners were no longer just destinations, but locations of atrocities. During the riots at least eleven innocent black men were ruthlessly tortured and lynched.

There was no plea for the humane treatment of Abraham Franklin, a crippled invalid who was dragged out of bed and lynched from a lamppost on the corner of Twenty-Seventh Street and Seventh Avenue. New York's black press relayed the gruesome details of Franklin's lynching. The *Anglo-African* stated that rioters cut "bits of flesh out of his legs and afterwards set fire to him! All this was done beneath the eyes of his widowed mother."

Franklin's mutilated corpse was dragged through the street by a sixteen-year-old boy. Many of the rioters' most despicable acts were performed by boys who were not yet draft age eligible.

Order was finally restored when battle-weary troops returned from Gettysburg to take control of the city. During the week of rioting, 119 people were killed,[11] thousands more were injured, and property damages were estimated to be more than one million dollars. To this day, the New York City Draft Riots remain the bloodiest civil resistance in American history. In all, only sixty-seven of those indicted were convicted of a crime, with most of them receiving light sentences.

The fears of the mob were never realized. Ninety-eight percent of those drafted in New York never served. Through various means, the city appropriated five million dollars of public funds for draft exemptions. Overall, the federal government raised more than fifteen million dollars in fees this way. There were no such special appeals for mistreated blacks, who were hard-pressed to recover any loss of property. However, the more than one hundred local businesses that formed the Committee of Merchants for the Relief of Colored People distributed forty thousand dollars to twenty-five hundred applicants, according to the *Pacific Appeal*.

Twenty percent of Manhattan's black population left, never to return. Elizabeth and her family stayed. Those who endured read about the Soldiers' National Cemetery opening in Gettysburg that November. Edward Everett, the "Little Orator" from Arthur's teaching days, was the main speaker. President Lincoln was also invited to speak.

The spirit of Gettysburg carried over to Manhattan's Union League Club, which raised money for New York's first black regiment. Earlier, Charles Remond Douglass, the youngest son of Frederick, was the first African American to enlist in New York during the Civil War, volunteering for the Fifty-Fourth Massachusetts Infantry Regiment, made famous in the film *Glory*.

As if rising from the ashes of the Draft Riots despair, on March 5, 1864, the Union League presented the recently formed New York Twentieth Regiment with its battle colors at Union Square. From there, its one thousand black soldiers marched down Broadway to the Hudson River before a crowd of one hundred thousand well-wishers. They marched in formation. Banners and flags waving, they were dressed in navy-blue uniforms with white spats and gloves. It was the largest display of black power since the parades of Thomas Jennings's youth. As a show of support, the three hundred members of the Union Club marched with them.

The Twentieth Regiment joined 180,000 African American soldiers who fought for the Union cause and helped hasten slavery's demise. No one knew this monster better than Rev. Henry Highland Garnet, a former slave himself. On February 12, 1865, he became the first African American to speak in the Capitol. His sermon, titled "Let the Monster Perish," was delivered shortly after Congress passed the Thirteenth Amendment to the United States Constitution banning slavery forever.

Garnet's lament pitted simple good against evil and recalled the wishes of the country's founding fathers to end slavery. Like a wild beast, it needed to be destroyed.

> *The great day of the nation's judgment has come, and who shall be able to stand? Even we, whose ancestors have suffered the afflictions which are inseparable from a condition of slavery, for the period of two centuries and a half, now pity our land and weep with those who weep.*
>
> *Upon the total and complete destruction of this accursed sin depends the safety and perpetuity of our Republic and its excellent institutions.*
>
> *Let slavery die, give it no respite, but let it be ignominiously executed.*

With a Union victory in sight, he ended on an optimistic note: "Thus shall we give to the world the form of a model Republic . . . in which the burdens of war and the blessings of peace are equally borne and enjoyed by all."

But the monster would claim one more. While Manhattan healed from its wounds, Edwin Booth staged a benefit performance to raise money to place a statue of William Shakespeare in the recently opened Central Park. For the first time ever, the renowned Booth brothers—Edwin, Junius Jr., and John—would appear on stage together in Shakespeare's *Julius Caesar,* about the assassination of the Roman Empire's greatest leader. Tickets at the Winter Garden Theater went for an astronomical five dollars a head—nearly twice what singer Jenny Lind received.

The brothers argued all the time. Edwin probably told the story of how he saved the president's son Robert from being killed by a train in Jersey City just a few years prior, while John Wilkes would rant that Lincoln wanted to be king. Later on, a photo card of John Wilkes called a *carte des visite* was found in Lincoln's personal card collection. (*Cartes des visites* were 2.5-by-4-inch cards patented in 1854. People collected and exchanged them.) On November 25, 1864, the event finally came together. Edwin played Brutus, Caesar's murderer; Junius played Cassius the plotter; and John played Marc Antony, Caesar's best friend.

Each scene was met with thunderous applause. The crowd was so loud at first, people at the performance hardly heard the fire alarms and screams. Outside, it must have seemed like another riot was underway. Instead, it was a foiled plot by Confederate spies to set hotels across the city, including the Astor, on fire. In true Broadway fashion, the play went on. While Edwin and John garnered many of the cheers, Junius had one of the more fitting lines. "The fault, dear Brutus," Cassius said as he described Caesar's power over them, "is not in our stars, but in ourselves, that we are underlings."

Enraged by the failed hotel fire scheme, John Wilkes Booth left his brothers for Washington, D.C., and another stage.

Chapter XIII

Nell's Window

The remembrance came with my first awaking in the early morning—as the thought of you always does.

—Chester Arthur,
Letter to his wife, Ellen Herndon

To many, the exhilarating events of May 24, 1883, were confirmation of American ingenuity. For the twenty-first US president, Chester Arthur, the day was more of a homecoming.

Arthur's rise to the nation's highest office was as startling as it was improbable. Although a master of the New York political strategy of doling out jobs for votes, or the patronage system, he never held an elected office before becoming vice president in March of 1881. Six months later, he took the oath of office to become the twenty-first leader of the United States after President James Garfield died from wounds caused by an assassin's bullet.

Twenty months into his term, Arthur dedicated America's greatest achievement to date. Although it took fourteen years to complete, claimed twenty-seven lives, and cost fifteen million dollars, the "Great Bridge" was completed.

In the years to come, it would simply be called the Brooklyn Bridge. As the sun rose on the opening day ceremonies, it was viewed as a technological marvel. Spanning the East River separating Manhattan from Brooklyn, it was a sight few people ever thought they would see during their lifetimes.

By nine that morning, a massive crowd had already gathered at Madison Square Park near the Fifth Avenue Hotel. According to the *Brooklyn Eagle*, the throng stretched down Broadway where "the faultlessly dressed dude and the gutter snipe elbowed each other and crowded together toward the curbstone." Every New Yorker wanted to catch a glimpse of President Arthur as he made his way toward the new bridge.

Zack was back.

In 1871, President Ulysses S. Grant appointed Arthur as collector of the Port of New York. In this position, Arthur oversaw thirteen hundred Custom House employees. They tracked and received taxes on goods coming into the country by ship. The New York Custom House collected 70 percent of the revenue for the US government, making it the largest federal office in the country. (Among its staff was Herman Melville, who sought the mundane security of public service to supplement his writing income, just as his good friend Nathaniel Hawthorne had. Melville was making four dollars a day on the Hudson River docks twenty-five years after publishing *Moby-Dick*.)

Arthur's role at the Custom House gave him a salary of twelve thousand dollars a year, according to 1877 government reports.[12] Add to that substantial bonuses from recovered smuggled goods, and his annual take was about fifty thousand dollars. Because of the vast size of his operation, he was able to give political allies jobs for loyal service (donations) to the Republican Party. Whether or not the person was qualified for the position was another story. Called the "spoils" or "patronage" system, it helped keep a political party in office. It also handsomely rewarded those in charge. Arthur's desire for wealth along with his ability to find common ground made him a valuable asset to an up-and-coming US senator.

Roscoe Conkling was a flamboyant, athletic politician from the Albany, New York, region. Called the "Apollo of the Senate," he had a personality that lighted a room better than one of Thomas Edison's new incandescent bulbs. He and Arthur made the perfect tag team. The boisterous Conkling was out front paving the way while behind the scenes Arthur made the spoils system work and grew their power base. In many ways, Conkling was the antithesis of the Elder Arthur, but Chester followed him. Arthur became a man about Manhattan, smoking the best cigars, wearing the finest suits, and eating at Delmonico's restaurant. Where a saw and hammer were the essentials of a laborer's trade, Arthur's were back slaps, free cigars, and late-night brandies by the fireplace.

After Grant left office, President Rutherford B. Hayes came down hard on the patronage system. He ordered an investigation of Arthur's Custom House. The Jay Commission found that too many people were working there and some officials were corrupt. In its July 28, 1877, edition, the *New York Times* relayed the Commission's findings. "Some employees were incapacitated by age, some by ignorance, some by carelessness and indifference; and parties thus unfitted have been appointed." One auditor in the Appraisers department found "according to one witness of nearly 800 errors a month."

While no charges of dishonesty were proven against Arthur, he was forced into a humiliating resignation.

Death visited the Arthur camp shortly before Chester's promotion to the Custom House and then a few years prior to his resignation. In mid-January 1869, Mrs. Arthur died after weeks of a fatal illness. Malvina Almeda contacted Chester after their mother passed away, and he notified the rest of the family. In her diary, Malvina wrote down a scenario that would repeat itself all too often.

Just before dinner Chester came. I do not know when it was, but Regina said that when Chester saw Mother, he sat down and wept like a child.

According to Reeves, Elder Arthur was so overcome by his wife's death that he spoke of suicide. Despite that revelation, he remarried quickly, to the chagrin of his children. The Elder's new wife knew how to make a marriage work. They lived separately, and she kept him locked in a shed. The war years had been hard on the family relationships. The old man didn't approve of his son's lavish lifestyle so there were fewer and fewer visits home. When the end was near, Chester's sisters once again called him back to Newtonville, New York, to see their dying father. The two men embraced, with Chester promising to stay by Elder's side. His sister's diary reported that he didn't. It was back to Manhattan and all its finery. Reverend Arthur died on October 27, 1875, without his first son nearby.

President Hayes's policies did little to protect the rights of African Americans. Two months after taking office, he removed all US troops occupying the former Confederate States. He believed that promoting the ideals of civil rights without the federal army to enforce those laws would bring together North and South. Instead, it gave rise to harsher Jim Crow laws devised to remove the voting rights of blacks, and increased the political power of the "Old South." Many African Americans felt betrayed by his presidency.

Arthur's improbable comeback began when he was selected as Republican presidential candidate James Garfield's running mate in the 1880 election. In its June 9, 1880, edition after the convention, the *New York Times* stated, "The nomination of Gen. Arthur although somewhat unexpected, was received with marked favor." At stake were New York's thirty-five electoral votes, the most among the thirty-eight states. A Republican supporter at the Union League Club told the paper: "Gen. Arthur will enlist in support of the ticket the powerful political influence of the City and State." The country broke along party lines, the Northern states voting Republican, the South Democratic. Garfield and Arthur won. Just four months into his term, Garfield was shot while walking through the Baltimore and Potomac train station in Washington on July 2, 1881. During his trial the assassin, Charles Guiteau, was reported by the press as saying, "The doctors killed Garfield, I just shot him." Garfield lingered on for seventy-nine gruesome days of questionable medical treatment before dying.

Arthur was at home in Manhattan when the news finally came on a sultry evening in early September. It was just before midnight when a reporter knocked on his door with the telegram that Garfield was dead. Arthur locked himself in his office and wept. He was strongly urged to take the oath of office without delay. The task of finding a New York State Supreme Court judge at this late hour fell to Elihu Root, Arthur's friend and an influential Republican lawyer. Shortly after two the next morning, Judge John R. Brady swore in Chester Arthur as the twenty-first president of the United States.

The Arthur who brought eighty pairs of pants with him to the White House was not the same crusading civil rights lawyer who defied odds and helped a schoolteacher win her battle against oppression. He had become an operative, a risk assessor, building political platforms to garner votes.

It wasn't always that way. At one time, providing for his wife's happiness and every need was all-consuming for Arthur. Nell wanted more of him, less of Roscoe Conkling and the Albany legislature boys. As 1880 approached, they planned to spend more time together going to the theater and other events, but once again Governor Alonzo Cornell summoned Arthur to Albany for a last-minute emergency caucus to form legislative committees.

Nell begged him to turn down the trip and stay home. Still trying to rebound from his Custom House dismissal two years earlier, Chester felt compelled to go to Albany. The upcoming year looked promising. On New Year's Day of 1880, the *New York Times* did a front-page retrospective on Arthur's career.

Fed up and lonely, in an act of defiance on Saturday, January 10, 1880, Nell went by herself to a benefit concert and performed with the Mendelssohn Glee Club, the oldest and most prestigious men's choral group in the country. In 1880, it wasn't something a married woman of the upper crust would do. Yet she did. There was a time when she sang with Chester in the choir.

The Mendelssohn Glee Club had a full-time conductor and traveled to concert halls in Boston and other cities, where it performed for large crowds and to critical acclaim. Nell was among the club's favorite attractions. She was known as the "Virginia Nightingale," the choir's leading soprano with a "rich contralto voice." The night of the benefit concert was bitter cold, with a harsh, snow-tossed wind howling throughout the night. In spite of Chester, she went and waited for hours in the cold for a ride home. On Monday the thirteenth, the *New York Times* reported, she was "lying dangerously ill at her home, suffering from an attack of pneumonia of a serious character."

Arthur hurried in an unheated milk train all the way back from Albany. He stayed at her bedside for more than a day without sleeping, but it was too late. She never regained consciousness. Ellen Herndon Arthur died at age forty-two. Arthur was devastated by her loss. For months afterward, he was seen sadly trudging down Third and Fifth Avenues near his home in Manhattan at two or three in the morning. After winning the election, he bitterly commented to a friend, "Honors to me now are not what they once were."

Arthur's surprise presidency gave new hope to the black community whose hard-fought rights were being eroded. Various publications such as the *Bay State Monthly* sought to shed light on the unknown man in the White House. This caused renewed interest in Elizabeth Jennings Graham's old court case. During the thirty years since the trial, history had been cruel to both of them.

Elizabeth's husband, Charles, died suddenly at age thirty-five of an undisclosed illness on June 11, 1869. Her mother moved to Long Branch, New Jersey, in 1867 and ran the Empire State House. For several years she placed weekly ads in the *Christian Recorder* as the "Widow T.L. Jennings," offering six rooms: "Board by the month, week or day, reasonable rates. Warm and Cold baths." By the late 1860s, Elizabeth was no longer teaching in the city school system. It's been suggested that she became a private tutor for better pay, and for a good reason. New York City put very little of its education budget toward schools in black neighborhoods.

The erosion of civil rights continued under Arthur's administration, highlighted by two cases involving the first African American cadets at West Point: Henry Ossian Flipper and Johnson Chesnutt Whittaker. They were roommates.

As the engineer for Fort Elliott in Texas, Flipper effectively constructed a drainage system called "Flipper's Ditch" to control the breeding grounds for mosquitoes bearing malaria. All was well until some petty cash from the fort commissary went missing. According to the US Army archives, Flipper testified that the post's officers knew he kept the money in his personal locked trunk because the commissary had no safe. His commanding officer never mentioned during the trial that the missing funds were found on Flipper's white housekeeper and cook. The Army's judge advocate general recommended the charge be reduced. Flipper was acquitted on this charge, but dismissed on "conduct unbecoming of an officer." His military career ended only four years after graduating from West Point.

After Flipper graduated in 1877, West Point life was hard on Whittaker. His classmates ostracized the young man. Whittaker wasn't allowed to join study groups or socialize with any of the white cadets. He roomed by himself, unlike other cadets.

On April 6, 1880, Whittaker didn't respond to his call to duty. He was discovered in his room unconscious and tied to his bed. Associated Press reporters were quickly on the scene. When post commanders questioned Whittaker as to what happened, the AP reported the following. "During the night," replied Whittaker, "three men came into my room . . . One struck me with that Indian club . . . They then clipped my hair and cut my ears." As he struggled with them, one shouted, "Let's mark him the way we mark hogs." They proceeded to cut notches in his earlobes and carved the hair from his scalp with a knife. Whittaker also produced a note warning of the attack.

A military inquiry by the academy found that the wounds were self-inflicted and accused Whittaker of perpetrating a hoax on his own. The problem, Commandant John M. Schofield concluded, was allowing blacks to compete on equal footing with whites when they simply were not up for the task. Whittaker was expelled from West Point.

Both of these cases landed on Arthur's desk less than a year after he assumed the presidency. Perhaps knowing his own reputation for running a Custom House whose books were somewhat askew, Arthur came down hard for law and order in Flipper's case. He ignored the Army's top legal counsel's recommendation and ruled that the dismissal was justified.

Whittaker stood trial for a second time and lost again. This time, March 22, 1882, both Secretary of War Robert Lincoln and President Arthur concurred, the court martial was invalid on faulty evidence.[13] However, that same day, Lincoln dismissed Whittaker from the academy for flunking an oral exam taken in 1880.

For young black men, the outcome was the same in both cases. Two of their best were forced out of the armed services. Increasingly, policies were being stacked against them once again. Between 1870 and 1889, only twenty-two African Americans received appointments to West Point. Twelve applicants were admitted, but only three had graduated by 1889. It took another forty-seven years for a black man to graduate from the academy.

Some African Americans were wary that Arthur would continue the Hayes policies toward them. Among the most outspoken against the new administration was Timothy Thomas Fortune, editor of the *New York Globe*, a weekly African American newspaper. He was a child of slaves; the KKK once hunted his family. Fortune published more than three hundred editorials and twenty books. As editor of the *Negro World*, he influenced many aspiring African American writers such as Zora Neale Hurston and Hubert Harrison. He moved to Manhattan in 1881, where he sold his own line of cigars and worked as a printer. Three years later, he wrote *Black and White: Land, Labor and Politics of the South* and was part owner of a publication that would evolve into the *New York Age*, one of the most influential black newspapers in the country.

As did the early newspapers from Thomas Jennings's time, these broadsheets gave a voice to the vast population of black Americans' suffering from social injustice, physical torture, and lynchings. Fortune's steadfast opposition to any form of discrimination attracted readers, as did his firebrand oratory. In an 1884 speech calling for self-defense, he shouted, "Let us agitate! Agitate! Agitate, until the protest shall awake the nation from its indifference."

Fortune questioned Arthur's tactics in trying to bring independent white Southerners into the Republican Party. He felt the black vote was taken for granted by the Republicans while their equality and political needs were sacrificed for white Southern concerns. African Americans were not protected at the voting booth, nor were they appointed to the same number of powerful jobs other political groups received. "Arthur combines the weakness of his predecessors without possessing their slim stock of virtues," Fortune stated.

Elizabeth Jennings Graham was asked by Fortune to meet with the president and to speak out against his policies. She refused Fortune's offer on both counts.

After Nell's death, the move to the White House was particularly hard on Arthur's ten-year-old daughter, Nellie. After Garfield died, there was no mechanism in place to confirm a new vice president. Arthur was now it. His son Alan was away at Princeton and unavailable to assist with Nellie. He asked his youngest sister, Mary Arthur McElroy, to serve as First Lady for several months out of the year and to help raise his precocious daughter.

Precocious Nellie Arthur delighted the press looking for any good news out of her father's administration.
LIBRARY OF CONGRESS

The widowed president was also starting a voyage of his own. Arthur began putting his stamp upon the office. He brought a new touch of class to a White House known more for having livestock on its lawns than heads of state in its halls. He hired Louis C. Tiffany, the son of one of his signature clients, to oversee the renovation. Twenty-four wagons of furnishings were hauled out and replaced with finery from around the world, quickly earning the new president the nickname "Elegant Arthur." Over the course of his shortened term, he held about fifty state dinners. These lavish events went on for hours, serving twenty-one courses while musicians entertained guests. Years later, the *New York Times* reported that one such banquet had 378 glasses on the table. Arthur took equal care of himself. Wearing only New York tailored suits, he changed outfits sometimes three or four times a day.

Arthur had a contentious relationship with the press and valued his family's privacy above all else. He famously told a prying visitor, "Madam, I may be President of the United States but my private life is nobody's damned business." That went doubly for Miss Nellie, who thought the White House "too big and lonesome," according to the *Wilmington Morning News*, January 12, 1882. With little else to celebrate about the Arthur presidency, and little coming from the man himself, the press took to little Nellie and her escapades. They covered her tea parties with friends as if they were heads of state. The construction of her dollhouse may as well have been the Brooklyn Bridge. Likewise, Alan, or Chester Jr., was the epitome of an 1880s college man. He was two inches taller than his father, handsome, and athletic. He was good at the up-and-coming sport of baseball and threw wild parties at the White House that went on until two or three in the morning.

Arthur benefited from these limited glimpses into his children's lives. After all, anyone who could raise such children couldn't be all that bad, could they? If Alan lacked a social conscience, Nellie made up for it. In the fall of 1883, she started a Christmas Club for kids. The collected funds were used to throw a charity ball for underprivileged children. The event grew so large that four separate balls had to be held to accommodate interest. More than two thousand homeless children were helped through these events, according to the *Washington Evening Star*, December 29, 1883.

Even after Arthur left the White House, Nellie returned to Washington, D.C., for many years to lend a hand with the Christmas Club. Although too young, and without the right to vote, she might have won an election if she ran for office.

The Arthur presidency was far from just a photo-op stroll to Nellie's dollhouse. There were twenty years of backroom deals and political vendettas lurking in the shadows. Conkling never wanted Arthur to run for higher office. When the campaign to draft Grant for another presidential run failed at the 1880 convention, in retaliation Conkling wanted the whole Republican ticket to fail. With much trepidation, Arthur approached Conkling about being drafted for the vice presidential slot. "Well sir, you should drop it as you would a red hot shoe from the forge," replied Conkling.

For Arthur, this was a chance at redemption after the Custom House scandal. Even a failed run would help restore his reputation. Conkling would have none of it. The two argued, with Arthur standing up to his boss for perhaps the first time and finally declaring, "Senator Conking, I shall accept the nomination, and I shall carry with me the majority of the delegation."

Early on, the anti-Arthur faction hit hard, accusing him of not being a natural-born citizen of the United States.

The initial rumors that Arthur was born in Ireland were quickly shrugged off. However, after Garfield was wounded, reports that Arthur was born fifteen miles north of his Vermont home in Quebec, Canada, also garnered much attention. The Arthur birther faction was led by Brooklyn lawyer Arthur P. Hinman, who was hired by the Democratic Party to investigate his background. Hinman jerry-rigged a story that basically said there were two Chester Arthurs, one with a middle name of Allan, the other Abell.

It didn't help that all those directly involved in Chester's birth who could respond to the rumors had passed on.

So many readers of the ***Sun*** in New York City were concerned about this rumor, the broadsheet felt compelled to send a reporter on a fact-finding mission to New England. On Wednesday, September 21, 1881, the ***Sun*** printed its lengthy front-page findings about Arthur next to Garfield's death notice with this final word on the subject.

> *In order to dispel the doubt about the President's middle name a gentleman intimately acquainted with the President's life and family and of so high political position that his reputation is more than national, was asked for an explanation. He said without a moment's hesitation that the President was named Chester after Dr. Chester Abell. Allan was the name of his grandfather on his father's side, and his father gave him Allan* [sic] *for a middle name in order to have both families represented in the full name. Dr. Chester Abell having been at relative of William Arthur's wife. This gentleman says he had seen in the Arthur family bible and in William Arthur's handwriting this record:*
>
> *Chester Allan Arthur, born in Fairfield, Franklin County, Vt., October 5, 1830.*

Hinman published his findings, *How a British Subject Became President of the United States*, in 1884, just in time for the next election cycle. As Reeves pointed out, Hinman lost track of his Arthurs. Chester's sister Annie was born on January 1, 1828. Hinman claimed the Canadian Arthur was born in March of that year. It wouldn't have been possible for his mother to sandwich another child in so soon. It also seems doubtful that Elder Arthur would have done a celebratory jig if he had already had a son who died. The birther furor subsided when Arthur lost the 1884 Republican nomination.

Perhaps the most extraordinary episode in Arthur's presidency had nothing to do with politics but a kinship developed through letters. It all began on August 27, 1881, as Garfield lay near death. Half the country cringed at the thought of Arthur taking over the presidency; the other half thought he had something to do with it. A pall hung over the capital and country as everyone waited for the inevitable.

Arthur was used to getting letters that trashed him or urged him to quit, but this letter was different. It was an honest appraisal of the situation and filled with encouragement.

> *Your kindest opponents say "Arthur will try to do right" . . . But making a man President can change him! Great emergencies awaken generous traits which have lain dormant half a life. If there is a spark of*

> *true nobility in you, now is the occasion to let it shine. Faith in your better nature forces me to write you—but not to beg you to resign. Do what is more difficult & brave. Reform! . . . Disappoint our fears. Force the nation to have faith in you.*

The letter was from a thirty-one-year-old recluse who suffered from a spinal condition and deafness. Twenty-three of her letters were among Arthur's papers. Julia Sand lived with her brother Theodore on Seventy-Fourth Street in Manhattan. She asked no patronage or favors from Arthur except blithely for a visit one day. Her gumption and wit caught him off-guard. Sand saw herself as Arthur's "little dwarf," an ancient reference to the role of the truth-teller in a king's court. Whether Arthur was truly spurred on by Sand's cheerleading or he just found her frankness a refreshing diversion from the morass of Washington politics, something had changed.

For perhaps the first time in his life, he was untethered by the expectations of others. His father's moralizing was gone, Conkling now reported to him, and the wealth he sought for Nell's happiness outlasted her.

Nearly a year after her first correspondence, Sand got her wish on Sunday evening, August 20, 1882. After a disagreeable supper, she was stewing in her own juices swearing to never write Arthur again when there was a knock at the front door. Suddenly the president stood alone in Sand's parlor with top hat in hand, requesting to see her. No security force, bodyguards, or detectives were in sight. He stayed for about an hour making small talk with the bevy of relatives who happened by that night. As Arthur put on his hat, Julia asked him whether he had forgiven her for some of the harsh things she had written in her letters. "No," he said with a grin.

Arthur was full of surprises for the rest of the country too. In 1883, he signed the Pendleton Civil Service Reform Act. The law ended the patronage system that raised Arthur to power and promoted only federal workers who earned it by performing well. Competitive exams for jobs were also enacted. The move stunned Conkling and the political machine that put Arthur in power. An able administrator, Arthur also gave the country standard time zones to improve rail travel and fought postal fraud. He began modernizing the US Navy by working with Congress to pass the Navy Act of 1883, which added three steel battle cruisers to a fleet of wood-hulled ships. His quiet, dignified manner seemed to grow on a nation that wanted to forget the Civil War and Reconstruction and get on with life.

That national life still didn't include all Americans. During Arthur's term, the Chinese Exclusion Act was signed into law. It banned all Chinese laborers from entering the country for ten years. Those nonlaborers who still wanted to immigrate had to obtain a certificate of eligibility from the Chinese government. Although Arthur was against the act, he couldn't stop its passage.

Likewise, in 1883, when the Supreme Court declared that the Civil Rights Act of 1875 violated states' rights, the president harshly voiced his disagreement to Congress. "It was the special purpose of this amendment to insure to members of the colored race the full enjoyment of civil and political rights," wrote Arthur in his third address to Congress in December 1883. He ended by asking Congress to pass legislation to "lawfully supplement the guarantees which the Constitution affords."

It's a call they wouldn't answer until 1957.

Another group dropped in to see President Arthur on March 6, 1884. It was Susan B. Anthony and about a hundred delegates from a women's suffrage convention. In return for their support in the next election, they wanted Arthur to recommend a Constitutional amendment for women to vote. When asked by Anthony if women should have full and equal rights, Arthur responded, "We should probably differ on the details of that question."

Politics weren't on center stage the balmy morning that President Arthur's carriage and twenty-four others headed toward the Chatham Street entrance to the Great Bridge. A sentimental man, he must have recalled that this was the very street that launched his career thirty years earlier with the fight against the Third Avenue Railroad. We don't know if Elizabeth turned out to see the aged legal warrior from her youth, but if she did, she wouldn't have been disappointed. Wearing a long black frock coat and white vest jacket, Arthur looked every bit the part of a distinguished statesman. His tall beaver skin top hat never seemed to stay on his head as he waved it constantly at the roaring crowd. The rapturous welcome from the streets he loved chorused around him.

After the ceremony, Arthur strode onto the bridge with New York City mayor Franklin Edson. A step behind them, Governor Grover Cleveland waddled to keep up. (In 1885, he would replace Arthur in the White House.) The procession neared the midpoint of the ramp toward the New York tower. The steel cables draped from it like rigging on a clipper ship. According to the *New York Herald*, the group suddenly stopped. "What a beautiful sight!" the president said to Mayor Edson. "Look at the tops of those houses. I have never seen anything like this before."

As the pageant reached the other side, Brooklyn mayor Seth Low greeted them. They had spanned an "aqueous Broadway," as one reporter put it, arriving "dry shod" on the other side. The band played "Hail to the Chief" nonstop. Cannons fired, ships blew their whistles, and church bells rang throughout the day. That evening a lavish banquet was held at the Brooklyn Academy for Music as fireworks and celebrations lasted until dawn.

It was now the people's bridge, and anyone who could pay the one-cent fare could use it. People from all walks of life—businessmen, laborers, musicians, teachers—made their way across the span. It's estimated that some hundred fifty thousand residents finished the trip on that first day alone. They took with them not only their belongings but their ideas too. Americans were on the move like never before. New inventions such as the telephone, electric light, and phonograph promised to bridge cultures and bring people together.

If only for one day, Arthur was a robust symbol of that spirit, but he bore a terrible secret. He was slowly dying of an incurable illness. Early in his term, Arthur developed Bright's disease, a term used to describe general kidney failure. Symptoms included severe back pain, vomiting, and fever. Attacks came on suddenly and sometimes lasted for days. It took Arthur a week to gain enough strength to return to Washington after the Brooklyn celebration. Not wanting to alarm the county, the president became even more distant from the press. He often didn't appear for business until the afternoon, leading critics to comment that his administration was lazy and uncaring.

In July of 1883, President Arthur was approached about creating a memorial to his wife in St. John's Episcopal Church, known as "the Church of the Presidents." It was also Nell's church as a child, and she sang there often. Arthur selected a memorial window on the south transept, or short part, of the cross-shaped church. He chose not to live in the Presidential Suite at the White House. Instead, his second-floor quarters were on the north side of the residence. From there he would be able to see the new memorial from his bedroom window.

The Ellen Herndon Arthur memorial was a traditional symbol of the Resurrection, with two stained glass panels showing an empty tomb. When it was completed, the church staff made sure they left the lights near Nell's window on so it could be the last thing the president saw before retiring. Every night, Arthur stared across the darkened landscape toward Lafayette Park at the glowing green, red, and gold memories of Nell.

President Arthur suffered in silence with Bright's disease during his time in office. LIBRARY OF CONGRESS

Chapter XIV

To Exercise Their Senses

Children are like tiny flowers; they are varied and need care, but each is beautiful alone and glorious when seen in the community of peers.

—Friedrich Fröbel,
The Education of Man

On June 4, 1890, Timothy Thomas Fortune had a meeting at the Standard Theater on Broadway near Thirty-Third Street. It was a busy afternoon in Manhattan. The New York Giants were beating the Brooklyn Bridegrooms 4-1 uptown at the Polo Grounds. Burlington was about to win the twenty-fourth Belmont Stakes, and the US population was pushing past sixty-two million.

Fortune felt parched as he walked toward the elevated railway, so he stopped in Trainor's Hotel on the corner of Sixth Avenue. He sat down quietly at the bar and politely ordered a cold beer.

"We have no accommodations for colored people," the bartender said.

Fortune insisted he had a right to be served. The bartender sent him to the café, where James Ennis, the manager, was having lunch. Ennis ordered Fortune to leave at once. When Fortune refused, Ennis called for the police. The officer said there was nothing he could do because no disorderly conduct had taken place. However, if they threw Fortune out of the hotel, the police could arrest him. As many early civil rights leaders did, Fortune stood his ground. The manager and bartender "laid violent hands upon" Fortune and physically removed him from the premises. He was immediately arrested. According to the *New York Times*, after he spent three hours in lockup, his friends posted bail.

The following morning in the Jefferson Market Courthouse, the charges were dismissed because of insufficient evidence. Fortune wasted no time in suing James Trainor and his hotel for assault, battery, and unlawful imprisonment. Going against the legal advice of the day, Fortune hired an African American attorney, T. McCants Stewart, to represent him before an all-white jury. Stewart filed a suit for ten thousand dollars in the Supreme Court.

But lawsuits take money, of which the militant journalist had little. Six years earlier, Fortune unsuccessfully asked Elizabeth Jennings Graham to denounce Chester Arthur's administration for "selling out" African Americans. This time she took up Fortune's cause.

In a September 20, 1890, letter in the *New York Age* titled "New York's Lack of Spirit," Jennings Graham admonished an apathetic black community for not rallying to Fortune's aid with financial support in a case that would benefit them. In the letter, she notes that her father made a similar public plea for funds in her discrimination case, but only collected seven dollars. Her father paid the rest of her trial fees out of his own pocket.

> *When the ejection of the undersigned from the Third Avenue railroad was presented by Thomas L. Jennings, deceased, in times that tried men's souls and women's likewise, if our voyance was required to remote parts of the city, the matter being one which challenged debate to our interests of the colored people, as an appeal for assistance was circulated broadcast. Many objections were raised for not responding but the most prevenient was that the course pursued might be deemed a conspiracy. The plaintiff belonging to many public spirited men of his generation sought the counsel of Lawyers Culver, Parker and Arthur (late ex-President) pushed their suit unaided and alone. The result was victory . . . Seven dollars was the result of the appeal.*

Elizabeth then gave several examples of times when the black community coalesced over an issue and the positive effects it had.

> *It may not be inopportune to call attention one or two other acts in which New York has not been backward. In or about 1832, in consequence to punishment and insult meted to a pupil, in the Manumission Society in this city, a number of parents became indigent and withdrew their*

children. Another school was opened, Benjamin S. Hughes appointed teacher, and four of my brothers and sisters were the first enrolled. This was the nucleus of the colored teachers in the city of New York . . . Other incidents can be furnished, but the sequel is left to more able contemporaries. Owing our increased cosmopolitan population, educational progress, and change of public sentiment no comment is offered.

The jury awarded Fortune $1,016.23 in damages from the hotel. Trainor appealed the judgment. On June 29, 1892, a three-judge panel reviewed the case. Ironically, Trainor's lawyer argued for dismissal because he wasn't able to probe the juror pool regarding prejudices they might harbor against establishments selling alcohol (Fortune's lawyer wasn't allowed to ask questions about race either). The hotel also claimed it wasn't liable for Ennis's actions, just as the Third Avenue Railroad tried to say it didn't have control over its conductor thirty-six years earlier. All the judges concurred and affirmed the judgment with costs. Fortune won, as the *New York Times* proclaimed with the headline "Decided in Fortune's Favor" on March 21, 1894.

Fortune's militant stances often put him at odds with the establishment. He advocated for using "Afro-American" instead of "colored" as a way for blacks to express their race and ethnicity. Fortune had a tumultuous twelve-year association with Booker T. Washington, serving as his advisor, editor, and as ghostwriter of his first autobiography. He also established important civil rights groups such as the National Afro-American Council, which set the stage for the NAACP to emerge a decade later. Supreme Court justice Thurgood Marshall was an admirer of Fortune's brave journalism.

Twenty-plus years before Fortune's trial, Elizabeth's mother returned to her Broome Street home and Elizabeth became acquainted with a former slave who escaped from Alabama to Mexico. He may have learned his trade in Belize, where the British used slaves to harvest and ship lumber. After establishing a life for himself in Mexico, Edward H. Wright moved to Manhattan and started a mahogany importing business. Acajou, or mahogany, was used to make expensive furniture, musical instruments, and ships. It came primarily from Central America, Cuba, and Africa.

Edward Herbert Wright Jr. was also known as the "Iron Master" because of his steadfast determination.
COURTESY NEW YORK PUBLIC LIBRARY

Wright joined the abolitionist movement in New York City and perhaps met Elizabeth or heard of her family at a meeting. He had two boys and a girl before his wife died giving birth to their youngest, Esther, in 1866. Wright and Graham, both now widowed, were engaged to be married. In November 1870, Wright left on a voyage to purchase mahogany, probably on the west coast of Africa. Before leaving, he checked his four children into the new Colored Orphans Asylum, relocated to 143rd Street and Tenth Avenue. This was a common nineteenth-century practice by single fathers who had to travel.

Tragedy struck Elizabeth again when her fiancé died on this last voyage. Little is known about Wright. His residence or importing business wasn't listed in any city directories from that time, nor did he take out any advertisements to sell his goods. With no record of a burial, it seems likely that he died at sea or on foreign soil. In case of his death before they married, the couple had arranged for Elizabeth to become the guardian of Wright's children when they were eligible to leave the orphanage at age twelve.

During November 1872, Elizabeth took charge of Wright's oldest daughter, Desidalia. Three years later, Edward Jr. was released to her care. Suddenly her empty home was filled with growing teenagers. Ezra, the oldest son, moved in with friends on West Thirty-Third Street. There is no record of Esther's release from the orphan's home. However, she appears in Census records as residing at the Graham household.

Busy as a mother, Elizabeth remained active in church affairs as assistant secretary for the St. Philip's Home, a refuge for the poor and homeless. Elizabeth's sister Matilda also served on the facility's Board of Managers. In 1875, Elizabeth and Cordelia Guignon started the Woman's Missionary Association of St. Philip's. The idea behind the organization was to support churches in Haiti and Africa. When they informed church elders of the initiative they took, their actions weren't looked on with benevolence. The two women sent an erudite apology, saying that "consent cannot be consistently asked for that which is already in operation." The male authorities grumblingly relented, and the association lived on.

In 1880, Desidalia married a well-to-do Cuban cigar maker and settled in Manhattan. Edward, who would have been roughly the same age as Elizabeth's son Thomas had he lived, followed his guardian's activist role.

Shortly after his sister's wedding, he graduated from the College of the City of New York at age seventeen. He taught for several years in the New Jersey school system before heading west.

Edward arrived in Chicago around the time the 1884 Republican National Convention was held in Exhibition Hall to learn about politics. Ironically, his guardian mother was there for the start of Chester Arthur's career; now Edward was there to witness its end and the beginning of others. While Arthur lost the nomination he didn't actively seek, a brash twenty-six-year-old New Yorker made a name for himself. Theodore Roosevelt Jr., whose father would have been head of the Custom House, replacing Arthur, had he lived, gave a speech supporting former Mississippi slave John L. Lynch as temporary chairman of the Convention, establishing Roosevelt as a voice of the future.

Four years later, when the Republican National Convention returned to Chicago, Edward Herbert Wright Jr. was a visible member of the local party. Soon he was the first African American to hold an administrative position in Illinois state government. By 1896, he graduated from law school and was elected as commissioner of Cook County. Wright was a shrewd politician who knew how to get jobs, services, and justice for the African American community. He organized black voters into powerful blocs that could sway election results. Wright earned the nickname the "Iron Master" for his determination.

During his long career, he upheld the Jennings tradition of using the legal system to fight oppression. Among his many clients was crusading journalist Ida B. Wells, who documented and spoke out against the lynching of African Americans in the 1890s. She also successfully sued the Chesapeake & Ohio Railroad for forcing her from a whites-only car in Memphis. (Wells lost her case on appeal when the Tennessee Supreme Court reversed the decision and ordered her to pay court fees.) Wright used his influence to have Wells's husband, Ferdinand Barnett, appointed the first black assistant state attorney in Illinois.

His finest moment came during the Chicago race riots. The trouble began July 27, 1919, on Lake Michigan when a raft carrying Eugene Williams and some school friends drifted from a segregated black beach on Twenty-Ninth Street into a white area near Twenty-Sixth Street. A white man, George Stauber, began throwing rocks at the raft, hitting Williams, who then drowned.

The police refused to arrest Stauber and prevented rescuers from helping Williams, who couldn't swim. By nightfall, black and white gangs clashed across the city. For the next five days, fighting erupted until the state militia restored order. The riots left thirty-eight dead, including twenty-three blacks and fifteen whites, and nearly five hundred forty injured. Thousands more were left homeless.

That August, seventeen death penalty indictments were handed down against African Americans. Despite documented rioting, no whites were indicted. As the first president of the Cook County Bar Association, Wright ensured that his group provided pro bono service to defend poor blacks who were arrested. They also helped African Americans collect for property damage and sue for personal injuries and death benefits.

Wright's memory lived on long after he died in 1930. In a March 8, 1958, *Chicago Crusader* editorial about Paul Robeson's book *Here I Stand*, the paper stated:

> *Paul Robeson has been one of the mightiest of all Negro voices . . . White folks are scared of this type of leadership. They feared it in Edward H. Wright in Chicago . . . In Paul Robeson they have met their match again.*

Today, the Cook County Bar Association still bestows the Edward H. Wright Distinguished Service Award on worthy lawyers.

After he left office, Chester Arthur's kidney condition quickly worsened. On several occasions he seemed near death only to rally once again. For the most part, he remained an invalid, rarely leaving his bedroom. He worked sporadically as the president of Psi Upsilon and for his law office. One of his last tasks was to reorganize the New York Arcade Railway, which had grand designs to elevate certain roadways and run trains underneath as a subway. He was its first president. Then miraculously, on November 16, 1886, Arthur was back on his feet. He took a light schedule of guests, wrote correspondence, and worked on several legal documents. Arthur commented that he hadn't felt this good in nearly six months.

That afternoon, he asked his son Alan to summon old Custom House buddy Jimmy Smith to assist with cleaning out his office. Three large ash bins were placed in the backyard. Arthur watched as all his papers burned. Papers are the lifeblood of any presidential memory, and it was as if Arthur wanted to wipe out his political existence. Filled with regret, he told his son he had done many things he wasn't proud of and warned him never to go into politics.

Throughout the day the flames licked high into the damp November air as the bins were filled and refilled again and again. We will never know what, if any, documents, letters, or court papers from Jennings's long-ago trial were destroyed in his purge. Arthur's quest for anonymity sealed Jennings's fate in history too. As dusk approached, the last embers in the bins reflected an amber glow on the bare stencil of trees. The next day, Arthur suffered a paralyzing stroke in his sleep. He lasted until the following morning when, the *New York Times* observed, "at 5:10 o'clock he turned on his pillow. All knew at once that he was dead."

Elizabeth suffered family losses too. In the summer of 1886, her sister Matilda passed away at age seventy-one. Earlier, in March 1873, her mother died of paralysis, followed by Sarah three years later. With her adopted family grown, Elizabeth had time to reflect on her own life. She followed the black migration from the Five Points area to Midtown in 1890. Taking up residence at 237 West Forty-First Street, she turned her thoughts back toward education and social causes.

After Fortune's trial, she was convinced more than ever that education was the key to change. Slowly the teaching profession was evolving. Larger buildings with multiple classrooms were replacing the one-room schoolhouses where Jennings and Arthur taught students. With smaller classes, the need for strict discipline and memorization gave way to independent thinking. Reformers viewed childhood as a developmental stage of life instead of a time to spend working. American philosopher John Dewey emphasized active learning as the best way to shape young minds.

Elizabeth was keenly interested in the work of educator Friedrich Fröbel. A self-taught German citizen, Fröbel fought against Napoleon at the Battle of Waterloo. Afterward, he dedicated his life to using education as a way to avoid the horrors of war. He thought the best way to prepare students for a lifetime of learning was for them to experience the positive aspects of school at a young age. Fröbel created games that used play and social interaction to teach basic skills. These exercises took place in a children's garden, or, in German, a ***kindergarten***.

The large influx of German immigrants to the United States brought the kindergarten concept to America. In the 1860s, the first English-speaking kindergarten classes opened for white schoolchildren. Elizabeth wanted African Americans to have the same opportunities to learn. Working with old friend H. Cordelia Ray, she did what the Jennings family was always good at doing—organizing.

Elizabeth established a committee with a board to explore starting a kindergarten for blacks. Many of its members were teachers from Grammar School No. 80 near her home. Mrs. James Morse was selected as president, and Elizabeth served as secretary. To meet the needs of the community, the committee insisted the school be free of charge. While everyone wanted the school, the lack of a building was a major obstacle for the group. Realizing her home was the ideal size and at the right location, Elizabeth offered it for the cause.

On April 5, 1895, the first kindergarten for African American youngsters opened its doors. It was more of a modern community co-op center than a traditional school. A detailed account of the school's opening was reported in the July 1895 edition of the *American Woman's Journal* by H. Cordelia Ray. The same issue paid homage to Elizabeth's long-ago legal battle. Established in 1870, the *Journal* was "devoted to the interests of Woman—to her educational, industrial, legal and political Equality, and especially to her right of Suffrage."

The article described a typical day at the school. Inside a large open classroom, a portrait of Fröbel greeted visitors with a quote explaining kindergarten as a way "to strengthen their bodies, to exercise their senses." The walls were lined with "pretty pictures of flowers, fruit and child life." A large backyard was turned into a garden where "little ones have planted seeds and roots and where they have an opportunity to exercise and play."

Elizabeth also taught sewing classes on Saturday mornings. The Graham Library was created to honor Elizabeth as the school's founder. Books were donated and circulated by people in the neighborhood just as the old Literary Society did sixty years earlier. There were also afternoon clubs and social work offered to family members. All the activities were paid for by voluntary contributions and services. The children also contributed funds to the school by performing plays and recitals. One such play at Hardman Hall on West Nineteenth Street the evening of February 14, 1896, was reported by the *New York Times* as being well received.

At a time when children labored in factories and the grime of industrial America was everywhere, Jennings's kindergarten must have seemed an oasis. By 1899, the school's reputation caught the attention of social-reforming photojournalist Jacob Riis. He told the school committee about a large empty store on West Sixtieth Street where another kindergarten could take root. Although in a blighted slum, the school was so successful that both black and white parents wanted their children to attend it. Elizabeth's kindergarten had a lasting impact on the area. It was still in existence in 1916 at 202 West Sixty-Third Street, providing "free education for colored children under six years of age," as noted in the *New York Charities Directory*.

Times and alliances were changing. After the Civil War, old friends became new enemies. In 1866, Susan B. Anthony threw down the gauntlet, saying, "I will cut off this right arm of mine before I will ever work or demand the ballot for the Negro and not the woman." Elizabeth Cady Stanton, who once stood with the early abolitionists, put the rights of white upper-class females above all. When asked if African American males should have voting rights, she said, "What will we and our daughters suffer if these degraded black men are allowed to have the rights that would make them even worse than our Saxon fathers?"

In the latter part of the nineteenth century, more often than not, the suffragette movement broke along color lines. African American woman led by Helen Appo Cook, Mary Church Terrell, and Ida B. Wells formed organizations such as the Northeastern Federation of Colored Women's Clubs and the Colored Women's League to promote black female suffrage.

These groups banded together to support their communities much the way their great grandmothers did in the 1830s.

On February 17, 1898, Helen Appo Cook wrote to Susan B. Anthony hoping to end the hostilities between the groups once so closely aligned. She recalled as a young girl accompanying her mother to Lucretia Mott's home in Philadelphia. "I was old enough to receive an impression, that was deep and lasting, of the noble character and lofty aims of the men and women there assembled." She then relayed her disappointment at attending her first suffragist convention and finding that "it was an appeal to prejudice as unexpected as it was disappointing; . . . it was like worshiping an idol and finding it clay."

Helen went on to point out that years ago her husband, John Francis Cook Jr., was part of the Republican Convention, nominating Garfield for president, when "there came from you a request to be heard." John Cook convinced the delegation to allow Anthony on the platform, only to be embarrassed by the old argument—how can you let "ignorant negros of the South" vote and not well-educated white women. Appo Cook ended with a plea: "I ask you in the name of universal womanhood to rely for the ultimate success of a good cause on appeals to the higher nature."

Her plea went unanswered.

By 1913, when five thousand women rallied for the right to vote during Woodrow Wilson's inauguration, white members of the National American Woman Suffrage Association refused to march with Wells and her black sisters. Seventy-five years earlier, they had locked arms together in defiance. Wells marched anyway, waiting for the objectors to pass before joining several white supporters.

By the turn of the twentieth century, Elizabeth Jennings Graham had outlived most of her contemporaries. All the others were gone: Douglass, Arthur, Culver, Stephenson, Pennington, and old Judge Rockwell. She was the last of her family members. By that time, Jennings was, as the article in the *American Woman's Journal* recalling her trial stated, "now quite aged." Like Arthur, she was suffering from Bright's disease.

That spring of 1901, the "Old Plantation" display opened at the Pan-American Exposition in Buffalo, New York. It recreated a romanticized "Old South," with actual cotton and cornfields worked by black men, women, and children who acted and dressed as slaves. It was among the most popular exhibits white people visited, and one of the most wrong-headed. After much protest, a display of African American life and accomplishments assembled by W.E.B. Dubois and others was begrudgingly tucked away in a building far from the main exhibits.

During the fair, President William McKinley was killed by an assassin, making Claes van Rosenvelt's distant relative Teddy Roosevelt leader of the United States. In 1944, African American sculptor Selma Burke met van Rosenvelt's other presidential relation, Franklin Roosevelt. For forty-five minutes the transplanted New Yorker sketched Roosevelt's profile on a brown paper bag. After he died, her engraving was used to produce the Roosevelt dime. Although the US Mint's chief engraver took credit for the artwork, until the day she died Burke said, "Everybody knows I did it."

Elizabeth spent her final days bedridden, listening to the laughter and singing of kindergarteners playing in her yard. Toward the end, she slipped into a coma. She died early in the morning on June 5, 1901.

Elizabeth was laid to rest with her family in Brooklyn, just as Arthur was with his outside of Albany. The world was on the edge of great change. Within two years, the Wright brothers would make their historic first airplane flight and Henry Ford would form a company to make automobiles. It would be nineteen more years before women could vote, and another twenty-seven years after that for a black man to break the "Gentleman's Agreement" and play Major League Baseball once again. One hundred years following Elizabeth Jennings Graham's death, the first black woman was awarded an Oscar. It took 107 years for an African American to be elected president of the United States.

During the intervening years, the Jennings legacy would remain largely unnoticed. History paved over their family's accomplishments, but Elizabeth was not to be forgotten.

Chapter XV

Shadows of Tall Buildings

If only because she started something far larger than herself she deserves a place of honor in the history of civil rights in New York.

—John H. Hewitt,
"The Search for Elizabeth Jennings"

In the fall of 1991, construction crews began digging the foundation for a federal office building in lower Manhattan. They uncovered not only layers of soil but layers of history as well.

About twenty feet below the surface, a startling discovery was made. The remains of 13 people were found under an alleyway between Broadway and Duane Street. Soon the graves of 419 people were unearthed. Estimates showed that 10,000 to 20,000 were likely buried there.

The bodies were part of a community of the dead that researchers always thought existed called the African Burial Ground. It was a place where slaves were laid to rest more than three hundred fifty years ago. Silent for so long, they were now speaking volumes about the city's past. This wasn't the dry facts of a distant time recorded in books. These were real lives revealed to New Yorkers for the first time.

Although deemed unimportant by their overseers, the unidentified children, women, and men carried a dignity that transcended time. Found in crude hexagon-shaped coffins facing west, they clung to the ornaments and symbols of their ancestral cultures. They were not unlike Americans today in so many ways. Suddenly New Yorkers were faced with a history few knew existed.

The need to understand the African Burial Ground led to a renewed interest in black history. New Yorkers wanting to confront their forgotten past sought out information about the city's African American culture and origins. That year, the Museum of the City of New York began a history club. Perhaps after reading John Hewitt's recently published article "The Search for Elizabeth Jennings," a group of sixth-grade girls put on a play about her life. After their performance at the museum's first history fair, the students circulated a petition to rename Park Row (formerly Chatham Street) after Jennings. The city never responded to them.

Elizabeth Jennings's place in history is equally easy to overlook. Some historians discount her contribution to civil rights because they say her victory only affected a single streetcar line in New York. Other events also helped minimize Elizabeth's accomplishments. The most important concerned a thirty-four-year-old shoemaker from New Orleans.

In 1892, Homer Plessy boarded an Eastern Louisiana Railway car. He was arrested for sitting in a whites-only section. Eventually *Plessy v. Ferguson* made its way to the US Supreme Court. On May 18, 1896, by a vote of 7-1, the Court upheld earlier verdicts for the railroad. The "separate but equal" policy that the *Plessy* decision supported became the rule of the land. The long shadow of government-sanctioned discrimination cast by *Plessy v. Ferguson* seemed to blot out any remembrance of civil rights gains from earlier times. For nearly sixty years, segregation held a firm grip on the courts and American society.

As the African Burial Ground Project gained momentum, it expanded its coverage to recover other parts of the city's black experience. On the hundredth anniversary of her death, the group staged a celebration of Elizabeth Jennings's life. At a graveside service, friends, extended family, and local historians gathered to honor her memory. Vandalism and neglect had ravaged the once proud family burial site. A memorial fund was started to restore the Jennings plot at Cypress Hills Cemetery.

In addition, local artist Susan Ackoff-Ortega was commissioned to paint a four-panel mural of Jennings's struggle. It depicted the events of 1854 and her trial. During the summer of 2001, the mural was put on display at locations throughout the city. Elizabeth and her family were finally getting the recognition they deserved. For safekeeping, the mural was stored in the basement of the group's headquarters at 6 World Trade Center.

At 10:28 a.m. on September 11, when the second Twin Tower collapsed, it gouged a deep crater in the basement of building 6. Everything inside, including Jennings's mural, was destroyed. That day there was no color in the city; only shades of gray covered lower Manhattan. The attacks resulted in nearly three thousand innocent lives lost. The total still grows.

Slowly the city recovered, as did the efforts to recognize Jennings. Picking up the work of the earlier students, the third and fourth graders of P.S. 361 wanted to rename the Pearl Street playground near their school in her honor. For the next year, the children collected petitions, went to meetings, and wrote to government officials. They too were turned down.

Meanwhile, other cities recognized Jennings's civil rights contributions. Each spring until recently, the city of Pittsburgh celebrated "Remembering Elizabeth Jennings Day." It gave out awards in her honor to "women who fight for equality." The celebrations took place at various churches throughout the city.

The students of P.S. 361 didn't give up their quest. Switching gears, the class asked that Park Row between Spruce and Beekman Streets be renamed. On June 15, 2007, a ceremony was held to dedicate that area for Elizabeth Jennings. It was a cool overcast day as the small crowd gathered near the signpost.

After a few words, the sign was ready to be revealed. The crowd began to pull on the cord to uncover the new street name. Suddenly the rope snapped, leaving the sign covered. Tim Allan, a white child, started to climb the aluminum post. Now an adult, he too works in the field of education. Lifted by his classmates and teachers that day, he slid the plain brown wrapper off to reveal "Elizabeth Jennings Place."

Afterlife

Are we fallen angels who didn't want to believe that nothing is nothing and so were born to lose our loved ones and dear friends one by one.

—Jack Kerouac,
The Dharma Bums

They say the third time's the charm, and in this case, it was a gem. Chester A. Arthur didn't live long enough to see his only grandchild, Chester Alan Arthur III. But if he did, it's highly unlikely they would have been kindred spirits. Where Chester lived for anonymity, Gavin, as he liked to be called, wanted center stage.

Without one, we would likely have limited knowledge of the other. Born and bred in sooty Manhattan, Chester II (also known as Alan) suffered from asthma and relocated to a 250,000-acre ranch in Colorado Springs. The cattle, mining, and timber from his investment ensured he didn't have to work a desk job like his father. His son Chester Alan Arthur III was born there on March 21, 1901.

While Alan's asthma improved, his marriage didn't. The third Chester was raised mostly by his heiress mother Myra, who was also an Eastern mystic and follower of "the Omnipotent Oom," an early practitioner of yoga. Like his father, Chester III headed to Columbia University, but soon dropped out, got married, and was thrown in jail for his involvement with the Irish Republican Army. He also had an affair with the British poet Edward Carpenter (who had an affair with Walt Whitman); starred in a silent avant-grade movie, *Borderline*, with Paul Robeson; and began a utopian beach commune and a literary magazine on the dunes of San Luis Obispo, California. He changed his name to Gavin after his fraternal third great-grandfather.

During World War II, Gavin served in the US Navy.

But it wasn't until the 1950s and '60s that his life really became interesting. Cut off from family funds, Gavin taught classes in San Quentin Prison, sold newspapers on the street, and prospected for gold. He began hanging out with the Beat Generation when he returned to New York City while attempting to write the Arthur family history. Pfaff's of Whitman's era was gone, but the dive bars Kettle of Fish and Caffe Reggio were there. Gavin was an early proponent of gay rights and was sought out by Alfred Kinsey for his study on gay sexuality.[14]

Meanwhile, in 1962, Gavin published *The Circle of Sex*, which melded his concepts of astrology and human relationships into a kind of Wheel of Fortune that spelled out intimate meaning to its purveyors. Gavin Arthur was now a guru, mystic, and astrologist on the circuit doing talk shows, newspaper interviews, and book signings. There was always that family history he wanted to write in the back of his mind, but he never got around to doing it. It was fairly well known in some circles that President Arthur's papers were destroyed. Chester Arthur II led inquirers to believe that the former president didn't write much anyway. After his father died of a heart attack at age seventy-three in 1937, Gavin found about two thousand documents and eighty bound books of press clippings belonging to President Arthur in a bank vault in Colorado.

Gavin had a bit of his grandfather in him, because he did a pretty good job of organizing the papers and having handwritten letters retyped. In the late 1930s, some of those documents went to Columbia University and others to the New-York Historical Society. According to Reeves, the rest were moved to Gavin's apartment in Manhattan and then back to the dunes of San Luis Obispo. Short of funds, he sold off portions of the papers over the next two decades to a mix of private collectors, various libraries, and the Library of Congress.

When Gavin Arthur died on April 28, 1972, he left all his family papers to the Library of Congress. They were stored in wooden fruit boxes in his apartment. Gavin broke the mold and was the last direct descendant of the Arthur Clan in America.

Precocious Nellie Arthur, whose antics delighted the presidential press, died young as her mother did. During surgery in 1915, she received a new procedure called a blood transfusion that didn't work. She was forty-three years old. Chester Arthur's town house on Lexington Avenue, where he fought for the Union and lived with his Confederate wife, operates as an eatery. On foggy mornings, his statue in nearby Madison Square Park appears to shed a tear for his long-lost Nell, while across the green Roscoe Conkling's bronze likeness glares at his protégé for eternity.

Andrew Haswell Green, the head of the Board of Education who banned Elizabeth from graduating with her teaching class because she was black, went on to become one of the most powerful men in the history of the Empire City. Known as the "Father of Greater New York," he piloted Central Park, the Bronx Zoo, and the American Museum of Natural History, among other projects, from concepts to concrete. Near the turn of the twentieth century, he realized a decades-long dream and consolidated the towns, villages, and municipalities of the region into the five boroughs of the Greater City of New York that we know today.

On Friday the thirteenth in November 1903, Green was murdered in a love triangle case of mistaken identity. The eighty-three-year-old was returning from a morning meeting when Cornelius Williams mistook him for another man. (It was discovered later that the man Williams wanted to settle his score with was John R. Platt.) Andrew pleaded for his life, saying he wasn't who Williams thought he was. The deranged man didn't listen and gunned down Green in front of his Park Avenue home.

Despite his innocence, the scandal involving an exotic black woman followed Green to the grave. The man who once fought to keep the races separate was guilty by association and forgotten. Until recently, only a lone granite bench in Central Park acknowledged him. Today, a rehabilitated section of East River waterfront bears his name. Anonymity turned President Arthur into a kitschy cameo footnote in movies and television shows such as *Bill & Ted's Bogus Journey*, *Transformers*, *The Simpsons*, and *Futurama*. His grandson would've been proud of the "old general's" new role.

Gold is lost but never forgotten. Using Bayesian search theory along with robotic equipment, a group of Ohio treasure hunters found Captain Herndon's SS *Central America* on September 11, 1988. The total value of the recovered gold was estimated to be more than fifty million dollars. However, thirty-nine insurance companies laid claim to the profits, stating they paid for the damages more than a hundred years ago. In 1996, 92 percent of the profits were awarded to the treasure hunters. Rather than pay his investors, the team leader took off with the dough. He was extradited to Ohio in 2015. To date, only 5 percent of the shipwreck site has been explored.

On August 18, 2017, the statue of US Supreme Court Chief Justice Roger Taney, the man who wrote the *Dred Scott* decision in 1857, had its own day of reckoning in the wake of public pressure to remove Confederate memorials. Under an almost moonless night, much like the one that began the Abolitionist Riots near Elizabeth's home more than 180 years ago, Taney's robed statue was separated from its granite pedestal on the grounds of the Maryland State House in Annapolis. The massive bronze figurine twirled as if it were grabbed by a claw crane used to pull toys from an arcade game.

Taney didn't join the Confederacy during the Civil War. In 1820, he freed the slaves he inherited from family. However, *Dred Scott* is considered the most erroneous and egregious decision the Supreme Court ever made.

According to the Southern Poverty Law Center, there are at least 1,728 Confederate-related emblems on public land across the country. Among the most popular memorials are Robert E. Lee, Stonewall Jackson, and Nathan Bedford Forrest, the first Grand Wizard of the Ku Klux Klan. Only twenty-seven of the thirty-six US states ratified the Thirteenth Amendment in 1865. Two states held out against abolishing slavery until recently. Kentucky finally ratified the amendment in 1976. Mississippi waited another twenty years. However, the resolution didn't take effect until 2013.

In 2009, Elizabeth Jennings Graham was included in the Topps American Heritage Card series as Topps No. 60. Her card was available on eBay for 99 cents. On March 12, 2014, Congressman Hakeem Jeffries from the Eighth District of New York (Brooklyn) proposed H. Res. 514—honoring Thomas Jennings as the first African American to receive a patent from the US government.

Despite eighteen cosponsors for the resolution, it wasn't enacted by the 113th Congress. (The 113th Congress is considered one of the most ineffective of all time, passing only twenty-two laws in seven months.) However, in 2014 that Congress did pass a law (H.R. 1071) that specified the size of precious-metal blanks used in the production of the National Baseball Hall of Fame commemorative coins. The following year, the National Inventors

Hall of Fame in Alexandria, Virginia, inducted Thomas L. Jennings into its honored ranks for his "Dry Scouring" patent.

Recently found buried in New York City's Probate Court archives was a document entitled "In the matter of proving the Last Will and Testament of Elizabeth J. Graham Deceased." The handwritten document was dated July 12, 1901, five weeks after she died. Elizabeth signed her will nearly a decade earlier, on January 22, 1891. Of the will's three witnesses, there was one of note: T. McCants Stewart. In 1891, McCants Stewart, a well-known and successful civil rights attorney, was representing Thomas Fortune in his discrimination case against a hotel bar.

Elizabeth left all her "household goods and personal effects" to an Elizabeth Smith and a Maria Simpson, along with sums of money for each. She left an additional amount to Smith and her husband William, who was one of the will's executors. There was also a trust that she divided in half, one part going to a nephew, Frederick D. Stewart, and the other half to the four Wright children who were her wards.

The American Heroes Channel program *What History Forgot* also produced a segment on Elizabeth Jennings's trial in 2015. Katherine Perrotta completed her dissertation, "The Elizabeth Jennings Project," in 2016. Perrotta cited Elizabeth as "an example of an underrepresented historical figure." Her study showed that Jennings's story helped pupils relate better to historical events and raised their awareness of the problems marginalized groups faced.

In 2018, the Museum of the City of New York opened an exhibit called "Rebel Women, Defying Victorianism." It celebrated four New York women who broke the mold in the nineteenth century and had an impact on our lives today. Along with Hetty Green, Helen Jewett, and Adah Isaacs Menken, Elizabeth Jennings Graham was included in the display for her activism and defiance. The exhibit made good use of her only surviving photo. Standing behind a chair, hands folded on its back, Elizabeth stares with placid anticipation as if waiting for the future to arrive, wondering perhaps if a not-yet-born generation won't have to fight to get on the bus.

In early 2019, the "She Built NYC" initiative named five new monuments, one to be placed in each of the city's boroughs to honor trailblazing women who helped shape New York City's history. The statues will honor

Shirley Chisholm (Brooklyn), Billie Holiday (Queens), Dr. Helen Rodríguez Trías (Bronx), and Katherine Walker (Staten Island).

In Manhattan, about a half mile from her last home, a statue of Elizabeth Jennings Graham will rise in the Vanderbilt Avenue corridor by Grand Central Station. The monuments are expected to be designed and dedicated by 2022.

Taller, newer buildings now cast shadows across Elizabeth Jennings Place and upon the museums and those who honor her. Although many people passing under her street sign don't know who she was, or what she stood for, they benefit from her sacrifices. The city that never sleeps is a better place to live today because she and her family battled oppression there.

They fought, and every American won.

Acknowledgments

One of the most rewarding and sustaining odysseys of writing *America's First Freedom Rider* has been the generosity of the librarians, researchers, historians, authors, lawyers, professors, and public servants I met over the last twelve years.

Invariably, after quizzical looks, sighs, and head scratches, all enthusiastically embraced the challenge of helping me uncover the lives of forgotten and marginalized historical figures. Without their dogged determination and expertise, this project would not have come to fruition. I'm eternally grateful for all their efforts and hope acknowledging them here brings some recognition to the great work they do daily.

Laboring in vain is the lot of any literary agent. Emily Williamson developed a knack for whispering into hurricanes and getting her client's message across. I'm always amazed and grateful for her fearlessness and friendship. To all the folks at Lyons Press, Rowman & Littlefield, you have my humble gratitude. Kudos to my crackerjack editor, Stephanie Scott. With a surgeon's touch and a lumberjack's whack she put the sizzle on the steak and killed all the darlings for me. Didn't hurt one bit. Honest.

It's always risky talking to attorneys. You never know when the billable hours start. Special thanks to William Manz of St. John's Law School; Ralph Monaco and Mikhail Koulikov from the New York Law Institute; Judge Al Rosenblatt and Bill Nelson, professors and legal historians at NYU Law School; Richard Tuske, NYC Bar Library; Marc Bloustein from the Historical Society of the New York Courts; and Jacqueline Cantwell, law librarian for the Brooklyn Supreme Court. An extra shout-out to patent historian Zvi Rosen, who generously shared Elizabeth Jennings's probated papers.

Historians are a collegial group, and many were an enormous help: Emilyn L. Brown, NYU; John Hepp, Wilkes University; Sarah Gronningsater from the University of Pennsylvania; Katherine Perrotta, Mercer

University; and Lisa Keller of SUNY Purchase. Thanks also to regional historians Jody Clark of Gardiner, Maine; Trisha Dolton, Greenwich, New York; Lynn Humphrey, the Timothy Thomas Fortune Foundation; Marcella Micucci, MCNY, curator of the Rebel Women exhibit; Kaitlyn Greenidge, the Weeksville Heritage Center; and Johnathan Olly, the Long Island Museum. To Andrew Unsworth, Susan Ackoff-Ortega, African Burial Ground Project, and Ken Rockwell for sharing his family history, thanks as well.

Good reference librarians are worth their weight in gold, and I hit the mother lode with every trip I made to these institutions. The NYPL's Schomburg Center was outstanding, as were the folks running the Pincus and Firyal Map Room and the Milstein Microform Room. I spent many Saturdays in the New-York Historical Society's research library, where Eric Robinson gave me the white-glove treatment (you can't touch some items without them). Hats off to my hometown library for reeling in faraway books and to Godlind Johnson of the Stony Brook University Engineering Library. Likewise, to Olga Arena of Cypress Hills Cemetery and Jamie Hammons of St. Philip's Church, cheers.

I'd be remiss not to mention Peter Aigner of the Gotham Center, who has boundless enthusiasm for local history, and my Wine Box Crew critic compatriots—Christine Alderman, Samika Swift, and Yolanda Ridge. To TM and MS, thanks for believing. To old buddy Stew O'Nan, who read numerous iterations of this manuscript and quite casually thought of the book's title, thanks, man.

My daughter Gabrielle reanimated my creativity and helped me see the world in new ways; she's always extraordinary. To my wife, Camille, who made it easy to go storm the castle, you had me at hello, and still do.

Notes

1. John Quincy Adams was the US secretary of state at the time. After his presidency he argued the *Amistad* slave case before the US Supreme Court and won.

2. Tompkins died in 1825, but his portrait was at the ceremony out of respect.

3. More than thirty-five hundred stray dogs were bludgeoned during the campaign as well.

4. Ownership of New York City was disputed until 1667, when the Dutch swapped Manhattan to the British for Run, a tiny island near Indonesia famous for growing nutmeg.

5. Kat Eschner, "The Horrible Fate of John Casor, the First Black Man to Be Declared Slave for Life in America," Smithsonian.com, March 8, 2017.

6. Warren Billings, ed., *The Old Dominion in the Seventeenth Century: A Documentary History of Virginia, 1606-1689* (Chapel Hill: University of North Carolina Press, 1975), 180-181.

7. In those days, judges were able to try cases that weren't part of their court.

8. The circuit courts were eliminated in New York state on July 5, 1847.

9. Roger B. Taney was the fifth Chief Justice of the US Supreme Court and wrote the *Dred Scott* decision.

10. A hogshead was a wooden barrel holding sixty-three gallons of liquid, usually distilled spirits.

11. Some estimates for the number of deaths went as high as 1,200 to 1,500, but 119 killed is generally the accepted number.

12. *House Documents, Otherwise Publ. as Executive Documents: 13th Congress, 2d Session-49th Congress, 1st Session, Volume 1* (Washington: Government Printing Office, 1877).

13. In 1995, President Clinton granted Whittaker a posthumous US Army commission. Four years later, he granted Flipper a full pardon.

14. David Sandison and Graham Vickers, *Neal Cassady: The Fast Life of a Beat Hero* (Chicago: Chicago Review Press, 2006)

Bibliography and Sources

Chapter Bibliography—Books and Articles

America's First Freedom Rider is intended for nonacademic readers interested in the subject matter, not necessarily scholars. To all the historians and subject matter experts who took time to share their knowledge with me, or send information, I'm eternally grateful.

PREFACE: UNHERALDED LABORS

Hill, Marilynn Wood. *Their Sisters' Keepers: Prostitution in New York City, 1830-1870*. Oakland: University of California Press, 1993.

CHAPTER I. GOOD OLD NEW YORK STOCK

Boston City Directories. Tufts Digital Collections and Archives.

Brawley, Benjamin. *A Social History of the American Negro*. Project New York: Collier-Macmillan, Ltd., 1921.

Gronningsater, Sarah L.H. "Expressly Recognized by Our Election Laws: Certificates of Freedom and the Multiple Fates of Black Citizenship in the Early Republic." *William and Mary Quarterly* 75 (2018).

Ham, Debra Newman. *List of Black Servicemen in the Revolutionary War compiled from the troop rosters of the numbered record books*. Washington: 1973.

Inskeep, Carolee R. *The Graveyard Shift: A Family Historian's Guide to New York City Cemeteries*. Orem, UT: Ancestry Publishing, 2000.

Johnson, Shontavia. "With Patents or Without, Black Inventors Reshaped American Industry." Smithsonian.com, February 16, 2017, https://www.smithsonianmag.com/innovation/with-patents-or-without-black-inventors-reshaped-american-industry-180962201/.

Levy, Leonard, and Douglas Jones. *Jim Crow in Boston: The Origin of the Separate but Equal Doctrine*. New York: Da Capo Press, 1974.

Nell, William Cooper. *The Colored Patriots of the American Revolution*. Boston: Robert F. Wallcut, 1855.

Pope, Jesse Eliphalet. *The Clothing Industry in New York*, vol. 1. Columbia: E.W. Stephens Publishing Company, University of Missouri, 1905.

Quarles, Benjamin. *The Negro in the American Revolution*. Chapel Hill: University of North Carolina Press, 1961.

Sluby, Patricia Carter. *The Inventive Spirit of African Americans*. Westport, CT: Greenwood Publishing Group, 2004.
Stiles, Henry Reed. *A History of the City of Brooklyn*, vol. 1. Brooklyn, NY: Subscription, 1867.
Ward, Samuel Ringgold. *Autobiography of a Fugitive Negro: His Anti-slavery Labours in the United States, Canada, & England*. London: John Snow, 1855.
White, Shane. *Stories of Freedom in Black New York*. Cambridge, MA: Harvard University Press, 2009.

CHAPTER II. THE WIZARD OF WHIPPLE CITY

Brisbin, James. *From the Tow Path to the White House: The Early Life and Public Career of James A. Garfield . . . including a sketch of the life of the Hon. Chester A. Arthur*. Philadelphia: Hubbard Bros, 1880.
Calarco, Tom. *The Underground Railroad in the Adirondack Region*. Jefferson, NC: McFarland, 2011.
Crocker, Henry. *History of the Baptists in Vermont*. Bellows Falls, VT: P.H. Gobie Press, 1913.
Feldman, Ruth Tenzer. *Chester A. Arthur*. Minneapolis: Lerner Publishing Group, 2007.
Greenberger, Scott S. *The Unexpected President*. New York: Da Capo Press, 2017.
Howe, George Frederick. *Chester A. Arthur: A Quarter-Century of Machine Politics*. New York: F. Ungar Pub. Co., 1935.
Karabell, Zachary. *Chester Alan Arthur*. The American Presidents series: The 21st President. New York: Henry Holt, 2004.
Lovegrove, Deryck W. "Particular Baptist Itinerant Preachers during the Late 18th and Early 19th Centuries." *Baptist Quarterly* 28 (1979).
Psi Upsilon Association of New York. In Memory of Chester A. Arthur. Special meeting, November 29, 1886. New-York Historical Society.
Reeves, Thomas C. *Gentleman Boss: The Life of Chester Alan Arthur*. New York: Alfred A. Knopf, 1976.

CHAPTER III. SLAVERY IN THE EMPIRE CITY

Alexander, Leslie, M. *African or American? Black Identity and Political Activism in New York City*, 1784–1861. Champaign: University of Illinois Press, 2008.
Anbinder, Tyler. *Five Points: The 19th-Century New York City Neighborhood That Invented Tap Dance, Stole Elections and Became the World's Most Notorious Slum*. New York: Simon and Schuster, 2001.
Asbury, Herbert. *The Gangs of New York: An Informal History of the Underworld*. New York: Random House, 1928.
Berlin, Ira, and Leslie M. Harris, ed. *Slavery in New York*. New York: New Press/New-York Historical Society, 2005.
Billings, Warren M., ed. *The Old Dominion in the Seventeenth Century: A Documentary History of Virginia, 1606–1689*. Chapel Hill: University of North Carolina Press, 1975.

Brown, Sterling, Arthur P. Davis, and Ulysses Lee. *The American Negro, His History and Literature*. New York: ArnoPress/The New York Times, 1970.

Burrows, Edwin G., and Mike Wallace. *Gotham: A History of New York City to 1898*. New York: Oxford University Press, 1999.

Commissioners of the Sinking Fund City of New York, The Wharves, Piers, and Slips of the City of New York, East River, 1868.

Crockett, Davy. *A Narrative of the Life of Davy Crockett, Written by Himself*. Philadelphia: E.L. Clay and A. Hart, 1834.

Eschner, Kat. "The Horrible Fate of John Casor, the First Black Man to Be Declared Slave for Life in America." Smithsonian.com, March 8, 2017, www.smithsonianmag .com/smart-news/horrible-fate-john-casor-180962352/.

Farrow, Anne, Joe Lang, and Jenifer Frank. *Complicity: How the North Promoted, Prolonged, and Profited from Slavery*. New York: Random House, 2005.

Foner, Eric. *Gateway to Freedom: The Hidden History of the Underground Railroad*. New York: W.W. Norton & Company, 2015.

Harris, Leslie M. *In the Shadow of Slavery: African Americans in New York City, 1626-1863*. Chicago: University of Chicago Press, 2003.

Hirsch, Leo H., Jr. "The Free Negro in New York." *Journal of Negro History* 16, no. 4 (1931).

Hodges, Graham Russell. *David Ruggles: A Radical Black Abolitionist and the Underground Railroad in New York City*. Chapel Hill: University of North Carolina Press, 2010.

Leadon, Fran. *Broadway: A History of New York City in Thirteen Miles*. New York: W.W. Norton & Company, 2018.

Levine, Lawrence. *Black Culture and Black Consciousness: Afro-American Folk Thought from Slavery to Freedom*. New York: Oxford University Press, 1977.

Raboteau, Albert J. *Slave Religion: The "Invisible Institution" in the Antebellum South*. New York: Oxford University Press, 1978.

Sante, Luc. *Low Life: Lures and Snares of Old New York*. New York: Vintage, 1992.

Singer, Alan J. *New York and Slavery: Time to Teach the Truth*. Albany, NY: SUNY Press, 2008.

Wilson, Carol. *Freedom at Risk: The Kidnapping of Free Blacks in America, 1780–1865*. Lexington: University Press of Kentucky, 2015.

Woodson, Carter G., ed. *The Mind of the Negro as Reflected in Letters during the Crisis 1800–1860*. Mineola, NY: Dover Publications, 2013.

CHAPTER IV. BOLD MEN OF COLOR

American Colonization Society. *Address of the Managers of the American Colonization Society, to the People of the United States: Adopted at Their Meeting, June 19, 1832*. Washington: James C. Dunn, 1832.

Browne, Patrick T.J. "'To Defend Mr. Garrison': William Cooper Nell and the Personal Politics of Antislavery." *New England Quarterly* 70, no. 3 (1997).

Burton, Eric. *Slavery and the Peculiar Solution: A History of the American Colonization Society*. Gainesville: University Press of Florida, 2005.

Carter, Ralph D. "Black American or African: The Response of New York City Blacks to African Colonization, 1817–1841." PhD dissertation, Clark University, 1974.

Diemer, Andrew K. *The Politics of Black Citizenship: Free African Americans in the Mid-Atlantic Borderland, 1817–1863*. Athens: University of Georgia Press, 2016.

Douglass, Frederick. *My Bondage and My Freedom*. London: Partridge and Oakey, 1855.

Garrison, William Lloyd. *Selections, from the Writings and Speeches, of William Lloyd Garrison*. Boston: R.F. Wallcut, 1852.

———. *Thoughts on African Colonization*. Boston: Garrison and Knapp, 1832.

Gosnell, Charles. *New York State Freedom Train*. Albany: New York History, 1948.

Headley, Hon. J.T. *The Great Riots of New York, 1712 to 1873*. New York: E.B. Treat, 1873.

Katz, William L. "African America's First Protest Meeting: Black Philadelphians Reject the American Colonization Society Plans for Their Resettlement." BlackPast.Org, April 17, 2015, https://www.blackpast.org/african-american-history/african-america-s-first-protest-meeting-black-philadelphians-reject-american-colonizati/.

Kerber, Linda. *Abolitionists and Amalgamators: The New York City Race Riots of 1834*. Albany: New York History, 1967.

Lossing, Benson John. *History of New York City: Embracing an Outline Sketch of Events from 1609 to 1830, and a Full Account of Its Development from 1830 to 1884*, vol. 1. New York: Perine Engraving and Publishing Company, 1884.

Magness, Phillip W. *Lincoln and Colonization*. Columbia: University of Missouri, 2011.

Ruggles, David. *The "Extinguisher" Extinguished! Or David M. Reese, M.D., "Used Up," by David Ruggles, a Man of Color*. Published and sold by David Ruggles, 1834.

Seifman, Eli. "The United Colonization Societies of New-York and Pennsylvania and the Establishment of the African Colony of Bassa Cove." *Pennsylvania History: A Journal of Mid-Atlantic Studies* 35, no. 1 (1968).

Swift, David E. *Black Prophets of Justice: Activist Clergy Before the Civil War*. Baton Rouge: LSU Press, 1999.

Van Arsdale, Isaac. *Biography of the Rev. Robert Finley*. Philadelphia: J.W. Moore, 1857.

Wilson, Carol. *Freedom at Risk: The Kidnapping of Free Blacks in America, 1780–1865*. Lexington: University Press of Kentucky, 2015.

CHAPTER V. SISTERS IN STRUGGLE

Bacon, Margaret Hope. "By Moral Force Alone: The Antislavery Women and Nonresistance." In *The Abolitionist Sisterhood: Women's Political Culture in Antebellum America*, edited by Jean Fagan Yellin and John C. Van Horne. Ithaca, NY: Cornell University Press, 1994.

Boylan, Anne. "Benevolence and Antislavery Activity among African American Women in New York and Boston 1820–1840." In *The Abolitionist Sisterhood: Women's Political Culture in Antebellum America*, edited by Jean Fagan Yellin and John C. Van Horne. Ithaca, NY: Cornell University Press, 1994.

Boylan, Anne M. *The Origins of Women's Activism*. Chapel Hill: University of North Carolina Press, 2002.

Chambers-Schiller, Lee. *A Good Work among the People: The Political Culture of the Boston Antislavery Fair*. Ithaca, NY: Cornell University Press, 1994.

Child, Lydia M. *The American Frugal Housewife*. New York: Samuel S. & William Wood Project, 1841.
Chudacoff, Howard P. *Children at Play: An American History*. New York: NYU Press, 2007.
Dorsey, Bruce. *Reforming Men and Women: Gender in the Antebellum City*. Ithaca, NY: Cornell University Press, 2006.
Griffin, Clifford S. "The Abolitionists and the Benevolent Societies, 1831–1861." *Journal of Negro History* 44, no. 3 (1959).
Holland, Jearold Winston. *Black Recreation: A Historical Perspective*. Lanham, MD: Rowman & Littlefield, 2002.
King, Wilma. *The Essence of Liberty: Free Black Women During the Slave Era*. Columbia: University of Missouri Press, 2006.
McHenry, Elizabeth. *Forgotten Readers: Recovering the Lost History of African American Literary Societies*. Durham, NC: Duke University Press, 2002.
Melder, Keith. "Abby Kelley and the Process of Liberation." In *The Abolitionist Sisterhood: Women's Political Culture in Antebellum America*, edited by Jean Fagan Yellin and John C. Van Horne. Ithaca, NY: Cornell University Press, 1994.
Porter, Dorothy B. "The Organized Educational Activities of the Negro Literary Societies 1828–1846." *Journal of Negro Education* 5 (1936).
Sterling, Dorothy. *We Are Your Sisters: Black Women in the Nineteenth Century*. New York: W.W. Norton & Company, 1997.
Stewart, Maria W. *Meditations from the Pen of Mrs. Maria W. Stewart: (Widow of the Late James W. Stewart) Now Matron of the Freedman's Hospital, and Presented in 1832 to the First African Baptist Church and Society of Boston, Mass*. Washington: Enterprise Publishing Company, 1879.
Williams, Carolyn. "The Female Antislavery Movement: Fighting against Racial Prejudice and Promoting Women's Rights in Antebellum America." In *The Abolitionist Sisterhood: Women's Political Culture in Antebellum America*, edited by Jean Fagan Yellin and John C. Van Horne. Ithaca, NY: Cornell University Press, 1994.
Yellin, Jean Fagan, and John C. Van Horne, ed. *The Abolitionist Sisterhood: Women's Political Culture in Antebellum America*. Ithaca, NY: Cornell University Press, 1994.

CHAPTER VI. ZACK COMES TO TOWN

Chester, Alden. *Legal and Judicial History of New York*. New York: National Americana Society, 1911.
Chester Arthur Papers, New-York Historical Society.
Fowler, John W. *Catalogue and Circular of the State and National Law School*. New York: Van Benthuysen Printers, courtesy New-York Historical Society, 1855.
Langston, John Mercer. *From the Virginia plantation to the national capitol; or, The first and only Negro representative in Congress from the Old Dominion*. Hartford, CT: American Publishing Company, 1894.
Manz, William H. *Gibson's New York Legal Research Guide*, 3rd ed. Getzville, NY: William S. Hein & Co., 2004.

McAdam, David, ed. *History of the Bench and Bar of New York*, vol. 1. New York: New York History Co., 1897.

Reeves, Thomas C. "The Diaries of Malvina Arthur: Windows into the Past of Our 21st President." *Vermont History* 38 (1970).

———. "The Search for the Chester Alan Arthur Papers." *Wisconsin Magazine of History* 55, no. 4 (1972).

Shelley, Frank. "The Chester A. Arthur Papers." *Quarterly Journal of Current Acquisitions* 16, no. 3 (1959).

Strong, George Templeton. *Diary of George Templeton Strong*, vol. I, *Young Man in New York, 1835–1849*; vol. II, *The Turbulent Fifties, 1850–1859*; vol. III, *The Civil War, 1860–1865*; vol. IV, *Post-War Years, 1865–1875*, edited by Allan Nevins and Milton Halsey Thomas. New York: Macmillan, 1952.

CHAPTER VII. CITY OF OMNIBUSES

Alfred, Randy. "March 18, 1662: The Bus Starts Here . . . in Paris." *Science*, March 17, 2008.

Benson, Lee. *Merchants, Farmers and Railroads: Railroad Regulation and New York Politics, 1850-1887*. Cambridge, MA: Harvard University Press, 1955.

Bishop, J. Leander. *A History of American Manufacturers from 1608 to 1860*. Philadelphia: Edward Young, 1868.

Brill, Debra. *History of the J.G. Brill Company*. Bloomington: Indiana University Press, 2001.

Kennedy, William Sloane. *Wonders and Curiosities of the Railway*. Chicago: S.C. Griggs, 1884.

Mohl, Raymond A. *The Making of Urban America*. Lanham, MD: Rowman & Littlefield, 1997.

The National Magazine: A Monthly Journal of American History, vol. 9. "The Railroad Men of America, John Stephenson," pp. 753–755. Western History Publishing, 1888.

Pierce, Harry H. *Railroads of New York: A Study in Government Aid, 1826-1875*. Cambridge, MA: Harvard University Press, 1953.

CHAPTER VIII. LATE FOR CHURCH

American Woman's Journal. "The Story of an Old Wrong." *American Woman's Journal* 9, no. 7 (1895).

Douglass, Frederick. *Frederick Douglass: Selected Speeches and Writings*, edited by Phillip Foner. Chicago: Chicago Review Press, 2000.

Hewitt, John H. "The Search for Elizabeth Jennings, Heroine of a Sunday Afternoon in New York City." *New York History* 71, no. 4 (1990).

McShane, Clay, and Joel A. Tarr. *The Horse in the City: Living Machines in the Nineteenth Century*. Baltimore: John Hopkins University Press, 2007.

Sweeney, Hillary J. "Pasture to Pavement: Working Class Irish and Urban Workhorses in Nineteenth Century New York City." *American Journal of Irish Studies* 11 (2014).

CHAPTER IX. THE TRIAL

Bloustein, Marc. "A Short History of the New York State Court System." Presented at a Seminar on the Unified Court System of the State of New York, Sponsored by the New York State Library, Albany, New York, December 5, 1985.

New York Legislative Documents, New York (State) Legislature, vol. 35, 1918.

Poore, Ben Perley. "Chester Alan Arthur." *Bay State Monthly* 1, no. 5 (1884).

Railroad Commissioners of the State of New York. Annual Report, vol. 2, 1856.

The Revised Statutes of the State of New-York: Passed During the Years One Thousand Eight Hundred and Twenty-seven, and One Thousand Eight Hundred and Twenty-eight: to which are Added, Certain Former Acts which Have Not Been Revised, vol. 1. Albany, NY: Packard and Van Benthuysen, 1829.

CHAPTER X. THE LEGAL RIGHTS ASSOCIATION

Katz, William Loren. *Black Legacy*. New York: Atheneum Books, 1997.

Levy, Leonard. *The Law of the Commonwealth and Chief Justice Shaw*. New York: Oxford University Press, 1957.

Lobel, Jules. *Success Without Victory: Lost Legal Battles and the Long Road to Justice*. New York: NYU Press, 2004.

Lynd, Staughton. *Class Conflict, Slavery and the United States Constitution*. New York: The Bobbs-Merrill Co., 1967.

Paulson, Timothy J. *Days of Sorrow, Years of Glory 1831-1850: From Nat Turner Revolt to the Fugitive Slave Law*. Milestones in Black American History. New York: Chelsea House, 1994.

Sterling, Dorothy, ed. *Speak Out in Thunder Tones: Letters and Other Writings by Black Northerners, 1787-1865*. New York: Doubleday, 1973.

Volk, Kyle G. *Moral Minorities and the Making of American Democracy*. New York: Oxford University Press, 2014.

Waldrep, Christopher, and Michael A. Bellesiles. *Documenting American Violence: A Sourcebook*. New York: Oxford University Press, 2005.

CHAPTER XI. THE GREAT SCHOOL WARS

Andrews, Charles C. *The History of the New York African Free School*. New York: Mahlon Day, 1830.

Civil List and Forms of Government of the Colony and State of New York: Containing Notes on the Various Governmental Organizations; Lists of the Principal Colonial, State and County Officers, and the Congressional Delegations and Presidential Electors, with the Votes of the Electoral Colleges. The Whole Arranged in Constitutional Periods, Weed, Parsons and Company, New York State, 1867.

Documents of the Board of Education of the City of New York. New York: C. Van Benthuysen, 1857.

Elementary School Journal. "Britain's First Nursery-Infant School, Elizabeth Bradburn." *Elementary School Journal* 67, no. 2 (1966).

Freeman, Rhoda Golden. *The Free Negro in New York City in the Era before the Civil War*. New York: Garland Publishing, 1994.

History of Education Quarterly. Back matter. *History of Education Quarterly* 14, no. 4 (1974).

Hodges, Graham Russell. *Root and Branch: African Americans in New York and East Jersey, 1613–1863*. Chapel Hill: University of North Carolina Press, 1999.

Mabee, Carleton. *Black Education in New York State: From Colonial to Modern Times*. Syracuse, NY: Syracuse University Press, 1979.

Manual of the Board of Education of the City and County of New York. New York (N.Y.). Board of Education, 1847–58.

Reigart, John Franklin. *The Lancastrian System of Instruction in the Schools of New York City*. New York: Columbia University, 1916.

Rubbinaccio, Michael. *New York's Father Is Murdered!: The Life and Death of Andrew Haswell Green*. Seattle: Pescara Publishing, 2012.

Rury, John. "The New York African Free School, 1827–1836: Conflict over Community Control of Black Education." *Phylon* 44, no. 3 (1960).

Superintendent of Common Schools, New York (State). Annual Report, 1847–58.

White, Shane. *Somewhat More Independent: The End of Slavery in New York City, 1770–1810*. Athens: University of Georgia Press, 1990.

———. *Stories of Freedom in Black New York*. Cambridge, MA: Harvard University Press, 2002.

CHAPTER XII. THE CIVIL WAR COMES TO NEW YORK

Bernstein, Iver. *The New York City Draft Riots: Their Significance for American Society and Politics in the Age of the Civil War*. New York: Oxford University Press, 1991.

Committee of Merchants for the Relief of Colored People. *Report of the Committee of Merchants for the Relief of Colored People, Suffering from the Late Riots in the City of New York*. New York: George A. Whitehorne, 1863.

Documents of the Board of Education of the City of New York. New York: C. Van Benthuysen, 1857.

Foner, Philip S., and Robert James Branham, ed. *Lift Every Voice: African American Oratory, 1787–1900*. Tuscaloosa: University of Alabama Press, 1998.

Gottheimer, Josh, ed. *Ripples of Hope: Great American Civil Rights Speeches*. New York: Basic Civitas Books, 2003.

Greenberger, Scott S. *The Unexpected President*. New York: Da Capo Press, 2017.

Harris, Leslie M. *In the Shadow of Slavery: African Americans in New York City, 1626–1863*. Chicago: University of Chicago Press, 2003.

Holzer, Harold. *The Civil War in 50 Objects*. New York: Viking/New-York Historical Society, 2013.

Howe, George Frederick. *Chester A. Arthur: A Quarter-Century of Machine Politics*. New York: F. Ungar Pub. Co., 1935.

Mikorenda, Jerry. "How the Slave Trade Died on the Streets of New York." *Gotham: A Blog for Scholars of New York City History*. The Gotham Center for New York City History, The Graduate Center, City University of New York, 2016.

Murray, Robert. *The Career of Gordon the Slaver*. Self-published. 1866.
Ovington, Mary White. *Half a Man: The Status of the Negro in New York*. London: Longmans, Green, and Co., 1911.
Reeves, Thomas C. *Gentleman Boss: The Life of Chester Alan Arthur*. New York: Alfred A. Knopf, 1976.
Reilly, Timothy. "Genteel Reform, Versus Southern Allegiance: Episcopalian Dilemma in Old New Orleans." *Historical Magazine of the Protestant Episcopal Church*, December 1975.
Soodalter, Ron. *Hanging Captain Gordon: The Life and Trial of an American Slave Trader*. New York: Atria Books, 2006.
Sutton, Charles, James B. Mix, and Samuel A. Mackeever, ed. *The New York Tombs: Its Secrets and Its Mysteries. Being a History of Noted Criminals, with Narratives of Their Crimes*. New York: United States Publishing Company, 1874.

CHAPTER XIII. NELL'S WINDOW

Cleveland Weekly Herald. "The Colored Cadet" and "Did He Commit the Outrage on Himself?" April 9, 1880.
Dehler, Gregory J. *Chester Alan Arthur: The Life of a Gilded Age Politician and President*. Hauppauge, NY: Nova Science Publishers, 2007.
Gawalt, Gerard W. *My Dear President: Letters between Presidents and Their Wives*. New York: Black Dog & Leventhal Press, 2005.
Greenberger, Scott S. *The Unexpected President*. New York: Da Capo Press, 2017.
House Documents, Otherwise Publ. as Executive Documents: 13th Congress, 2d Session-49th Congress, 1st Session, Volume 1. Washington: Government Printing Office, 1877.
Hudson, William C. *Random Recollections of an Old Political Reporter*. New York: Cupples & Leon, 1911.
Klugewicz, Stephen M. "How an Obscure Woman's Letters Transformed a President." The Imaginative Conservative, April 29, 2018, https://theimaginativeconservative.org/2018/04/julia-sand-obscure-womans-letters-transformed-president-stephen-klugewicz-timeless.html.
Lengel, Edward G. "Nellie Arthur in the White House." White House Historical Association, November 1, 2017, www.whitehousehistory.org/nellie-arthur-in-the-white-house.
Marszalek, John F., Jr. "A Black Cadet at West Point." *American Heritage*, August 1971.
Papers Relating to the Foreign Relations of the United States, Transmitted to Congress, With the Annual Message of the President. Washington: United States Government Printing Office, 1884.
Reeves, Thomas C. *Gentleman Boss: The Life of Chester Alan Arthur*. New York: Alfred A. Knopf, 1976.
Schneider, Dorothy, and Carl J. Schneider. *First Ladies: A Biographical Dictionary*. New York: Infobase Publishing, 2005.
Shelley, Fred. "The Chester A. Arthur Papers." *Quarterly Journal of Current Acquisitions* 16, no. 3 (1959).

Smalley, Eugene Virgil. *The Republican Manual: History, Principles, Early Leaders, Achievements of the Republican Party: with Biographical Sketches of James A. Garfield and Chester A. Arthur*. New York: American Book Exchange, 1880.

CHAPTER XIV. TO EXERCISE THEIR SENSES

Charity Organization Society of the City of New York. *The New York Charities Directory*. New York: Charity Organization Society of the City of New York, 1916.

Colored Orphans Asylum. Monthly Report of Children Discharged and Received, 1859–1885, vol. 1. New York Historical Society.

Emerson, Helena Titus. "Children of the Circle: The Work of the New York Free Kindergarten Association for Colored Children." *Charities* XV, no. 1 (October 7, 1905).

Gordon, Ann D., ed. *The Selected Papers of Elizabeth Cady Stanton and Susan B. Anthony*, vol. 6: *An Awful Hush, 1895 to 1906*. New Brunswick, NJ: Rutgers University Press, 2013.

Mikorenda, Jerry. "Beating Wings in Rebellion: The Ladies Literary Society Finds Equality." Gotham: A Blog for Scholars of New York City History. The Gotham Center for New York City History, The Graduate Center, City University of New York, 2016.

———. "Timothy Thomas Fortune: An American Agitator Looks for a Cold Beer in Manhattan." Gotham: A Blog for Scholars of New York City History. The Gotham Center for New York City History, The Graduate Center, City University of New York, 2016.

The New York Supplement, Vol. 19, Supreme, Superior, and Lower Courts of Record of New York State, June 16–September 15, 1892, *Fortune v. Trainor*. New York Digest: Including All New York Cases Reported from May 31, 1888, to January 25, 1915, *Fortune v. Trainor*, 141 N.Y. 605 1894.

Peterson, Carla. *Black Gotham: A Family History of African American in Nineteenth-Century New York City*. New Haven, CT: Yale University Press, 2011.

Ray, H. Cordelia. "The First Free Kindergarten for Colored Children." *American Woman's Journal* 9, no. 7 (July 1895).

Waldrep, Christopher, and Michael A. Bellesiles. *Documenting American Violence: A Sourcebook*. New York: Oxford University Press, 2005.

AFTERLIFE

Giaimo, Cara. "The Racism of American Monuments Goes Well Beyond Confederate Statues: A New Map of Civil War-Related Landmarks Is Only the Beginning." Atlas Obscura, June 7, 2018, www.atlasobscura.com/articles/confederate-monument-map-2018.

Lomax, John Nova. "This President's Grandson Was More Interesting Than You'll Ever Be." Vice, January 13, 2017, www.vice.com/en_us/article/pgp7mv/this-presidents-grandson-was-more-interesting-than-youll-ever-be.

Perrotta, Katherine Anne Assante. "More Than a Feeling: A Study on Conditions that Promote Historical Empathy in Middle and Secondary Social Studies Classes with the Elizabeth Jennings Project." Dissertation, Georgia State University, 2016.

Reeves, Thomas C. "The Search for the Chester Alan Arthur Papers." *Wisconsin Magazine of History* 55, no. 4 (1972).

Sandison, David, and Graham Vickers. *Neal Cassady: The Fast Life of a Beat Hero.* Chicago: Chicago Review Press, 2006.

Historic Newspapers

Most newspapers were accessed online via various databases such as the N.Y.S. Library System, the NYPL microfilm collections, and Accessible Archives.

AFRICAN AMERICAN PAPERS

Anglo-African
Chicago Crusader
Colored American
Frederick Douglass' Paper
Freedom's Journal
The New York Age
New York Globe
North Star
Pacific Appeal (California)
Weekly Advocate (N.Y.)

GENERAL PRESS

American Woman's Journal
Brooklyn Eagle
Chicago Tribune
Daily True Delta (New Orleans)
Gazette and General Advertiser
Journal of Commerce (N.Y.)
Liberator (Boston)
Long Island Patriot
Long Island Star
Metropolitan Record (N.Y.)
New Orleans Daily Picayune
New York Commercial Advertiser
New York Daily News

New York Daily Times
New-York Daily Tribune
New York Evening Post
New York Gazette
New York Herald
New York Mirror
Sandy Hill Herald (N.Y.)
Tribeca Tribune
Vermont Tribune

Index

F

G

H

I

J

N

O

P